Max Farrand

The Legislation of Congress for the Government of the

Organized Territories of the United States, 1789-1895

Max Farrand

The Legislation of Congress for the Government of the
Organized Territories of the United States, 1789-1895

ISBN/EAN: 9783744721523

Printed in Europe, USA, Canada, Australia, Japan

Cover: Foto ©Suzi / pixelio.de

More available books at **www.hansebooks.com**

THE

LEGISLATION OF CONGRESS

FOR THE

Government of the Organized Territories of the United States.

1789-1895.

....BY....

MAX FARRAND.

JUNE, 1896.

WM. A. BAKER, PRINTER,
251 MARKET STREET, NEWARK, N. J.
1896.

THE

Legislation of Congress

FOR THE

Government of the, Organized Territories of the United States.

1789-1895.

====

....BY....

MAX FARRAND.

JUNE, 1896.

WM. A. BAKER, PRINTER,
251 MARKET STREET, NEWARK, N. J.
1896.

TO

MY FATHER

WHO HAS EVER BEEN MY BEST
EXAMPLE OF UNSWERVING DEVO-
TION TO HIGH PRINCIPLES AND
DUTY.

CONTENTS:

I.

The Origin of the Public Territory of the United States.

When the First Congress of the United States met in
New York in 1789, among the first subjects that came
before it for consideration was that of the government of
the public territory in the west.[1] More recent surveys
have shown this territory to consist of some one hundred
and seventy millions of acres,[2] but then it was merely a
vast tract of unbroken wilderness, stretching north and
west of the river Ohio, and designated vaguely as "the
Northwest." How had the United States come into possession of this vast wilderness?

About ten years previous the great obstacle to the
adoption of the Articles of Confederation by several of the
smaller States had been the claim of some of the larger
States to the vacant lands in the west. By the treaty of
Paris in 1763 the English acquired the western country
as far as the Mississippi, but a royal proclamation in the
same year confined the colonies to the country east of the
Alleghany Mountains.[3] The colonists regarded this as

---

1. Quorum of House April 1, of Senate April 6. The question
of the government of the Northwest brought up on May 18. The act
passed for its government (see p. 14) was the ninth act of the First
Congress.

2. Donaldson: The Public Domain, p. 61.

3. " That no Governor of our colonies in America do presume for
the present to grant warrants of survey or pass patents for any lands
beyond the heads or sources of any of the rivers which fall into the
Atlantic Ocean from the west or northwest."

merely a temporary expedient to quiet the minds of the Indians,[4] and confidently expected that before long the lines of the colonies would be re-extended beyond the Alleghanies. This was not done, however, and an act of Parliament in 1774 annexed the "crown lands," the term usually applied to the land west of the Alleghanies and beyond the Ohio, to the royal province of Quebec.[5] The colonies felt that the possession of these lands was indispensable to their interests, and the Declaration of Independence putting things on a new footing, such States as had any claim asserted jurisdiction over the territory which fell within their respective limits. Virginia, Massachusetts, Connecticut and New York were the only States that had any legal title to lands northwest of the Ohio. Rhode Island, New Jersey, Delaware and Maryland, so situated that they never could expand in any direction, regarded with alarm a course which would not fail to make the claimant States[6] all powerful, as it would depopulate and impoverish the non-claimant States. They therefore hesitated to ratify the Articles of Confederation unless these western lands were to be disposed of for the benefit of the whole confederacy, or for defraying the expenses of the war. A circular letter from Congress[7] urging the necessity of a prompt ratification effected its purpose with all of the States except Maryland. By February, 1779, she alone stood out in her refusal. In May of that year there were read in Congress the instructions of Maryland to her delegates positively forbidding them to ratify the Articles of Confederation unless they should receive definite assurance that the northwestern territory would become the common property of the United States.[8]

---

4. Adams: Maryland's Influence Upon Land Cessions to the United States.

5. The Quebec Bill, referred to in the Declaration of Independence.

6. Especially New York and Virginia.

7. July 10, 1778.

8. Passed by the General Assembly of Maryland December 15, 1778; read in Congress May 21, 1779.

As the consent of all of the thirteen States was necessary to form the confederacy, this refusal of Maryland's brought matters to a crisis. The question was earnestly discussed, and early in 1780 New York set things in motion by authorizing her representatives to cede all her claims in western lands to the United States.[9] This act of New York at once changed the whole situation. It was no longer necessary for Maryland to defend her position, but the claimant States were compelled to justify themselves before the country for not following New York's example. Congress wisely refrained from any assertion of jurisdiction, and only urgently recommended that the States having claims to western lands should cede them, so that the only obstacle to the final ratification of the Articles of Confederation might be removed.[10] As a special inducement to Virginia, it was further provided a month later that Congress would re-imburse any State for the reasonable expenses it had incurred since the commencement of the war in defending its western territory.[11] Connecticut at once offered a cession of her western lands, provided she might retain the jurisdiction.[12] Shortly afterward Virginia yielded, and upon certain conditions ceded to the United States all her lands northwest of the Ohio river.[13] The Maryland delegates were then empowered to ratify the Articles of Confederation.

Two of the conditions imposed by Virginia were not acceptable to Congress. The one involved a declaration of the validity of Virginia's claims, and a ruling out of those of the other parties ; and the other demanded a guarantee to Virginia of undisturbed possession of the lands southeast of the Ohio. Three years later (1784) after long discussion, at the request of Congress, Virginia withdrew the obnoxious conditions, and made her cession absolute.[14] The next year Massachusetts ceded her west-

---

9. February 19, 1780.　　10. September 6, 1780.

11. October 10, 1780.　12. October 10, 1780.　13. January 2, 1781.

14. October 20, 1783, Virginia delegates authorized to make cession in accordance with request of Congress. Delegates made cession on March 1, 1784, accepted by Congress same day.

ern lands with the jurisdiction over them,[15] and in 1786 Connecticut did the same,[16] reserving, however, some three million acres on the southern shore of Lake Erie for educational and other purposes, which is now part of the State of Ohio, but is still called the "Connecticut Reserve." " *The Northwest" thus became the common property, the public territory of the United States.*[17]

Legislation under the Articles of Confederation for the Government of the Public Territory.

In Maryland's first proposition to give Congress sovereignty over the western lands, made in October, 1777, it was moved that Congress should have the sole power to fix the western boundaries of such States as claimed to the Mississippi, "and lay out the land beyond the boundary, so ascertained, into separate and independent States." This idea, repeated in the declarations and resolutions afterward passed by the legislature of Maryland, was adopted by Congress in the resolution of October 10, 1780. According to this all lands ceded to the United States should "be settled and formed into distinct republican States, which shall become members of the Federal Union, and have the same rights of sovereignty, freedom and independence, as the other States." During 1783, when it was evident that Congress would eventually become the owner of "the Northwest," it was resolved in Congress that a committee should be appointed to report a plan for connecting with the Confederation, by a temporary government, the inhabitants of the new district until their number and circumstances should entitle them to form a permanent constitution for themselves.[18]

---

15. April 19, 1785. 16. September 14, 1786.

17. On cession of land by the States, see Adams : *loc. cit.*, Hinsdale : Old Northwest, Chap. XII., XIII. Fiske : Critical Period of American History. Sato : History of Land Question in United States, pp. 192 and 193. *et al.* Winsor : Narrative and Critical History, Vol VII., Appendix.

18. Adams: *loc. cit.* p. 43.

a) Jefferson's Ordinance, or the Ordinance of 1784.

Thomas Jefferson, as chairman of that committee, on the very day that the cession of Virginia was accepted, March 1, 1784, submitted to Congress a plan for the government of the western territory, which, with some important modifications, was adopted.[19] It was commonly known as Jefferson's Ordinance, or the Ordinance of 1784. It provided for the artificial division of the ceded territory into States, in each of which the settlers were authorized for the purpose of establishing a temporary government to adopt the constitution and laws of any one of the original States, and to erect counties, townships, or other divisions, for the election of members for their Legislature. When any such State should have twenty thousand inhabitants they were to receive authority from Congress to establish for themselves a permanent constitution and government, and should have a member in Congress, with the right of debating, but not of voting. Provided, That under both the temporary and permanent governments they should forever remain a part of the Confederacy; should be subject to the Articles of Confederation and the acts and ordinances of Congress, like the original States; should in no case interfere with the primary disposal of the soil by Congress; should be subject to pay a part of the Federal debts in the same measure of apportionment with the other States; should impose no tax on lands the property of the United States; that their respective governments should be republican; and that the lands of non-residents should not be taxed higher than those of residents. When the inhabitants of any one of these States should equal in number those of the least populous of the thirteen original States, their delegates, with the consent of so many States as might at the time be competent should be admitted into Congress on an equal footing.

There were many objections to this ordinance. The first draft had included only the territory north of the

---

19. April 23, 1784.

Ohio, but as adopted it covered the country south as well as north, territory to be ceded as well as that already acquired. Jefferson himself was bitterly disappointed, especially because the clause forbidding slavery after the year 1800 was ·stricken out.[20] There were those who felt that it was somewhat indefinite to promise certain sections of country admission into the Confederacy as soon as their population should equal in number that of the least populous of the original States. If the original States should increase in population to any great extent, these new States might be prohibited from ever entering; and on the other hand, if from any cause the population of one of the smaller States should suddenly decrease, would not such an alarming increase of new States as that might entail prove dangerous? And then the ordinance was not a plan for government at all. It established nothing. It fixed the limits within which the local governments must act, but left the creation of those governments wholly to the future. In Vincennes "the local government bowled along merrily under this system. There was the greatest abundance of government, for the more the United States neglected them the more authority their officials assumed."[21] But in Kaskaskia the people petitioned Congress that any sort of government might be given to them. And so Congress proceeded to legislate anew on the whole subject. Between May 1, 1786, and July 9, 1787, as many as three ordinances for the government of the western territory were reported to Congress,[22] and finally, on July 13, 1787, the now famous ordinance of 1787 was adopted.

b) **The Ordinance of 1787.**

The importance of the Ordinance of 1787 in this discussion lies in its influence upon the legislation that fol-

---

20. Letter to Madison of April 25, 1784.
21. Dunn: Indiana, p. 188.
22. May 10, 1786; September 19, 1786, and April 26, 1787. Hinsdale: Old Northwest.

lowed rather than in its connection with what had preceded it. It is not, therefore, within the province of this paper to enter into the question of its authorship,[23] nor to attempt to trace the origin of its various provisions. It suffices here to say that as it not only undertook to make political organizations and to provide for the admission of new States into the confederacy, but also dealth directly with the rights of individuals, it was a very different instrument from any of those that had before been considered by Congress, and yet it contained the greater part of these previous propositions, and its phraseology shows how greatly it was indebted to them.[24]

The first paragraph provided that, for the purposes of temporary government, the region northwest of the Ohio should be one district, subject, however, to division by Congress. The second regulated the descent and distribution of estates, securing to the inhabitants the equal division of the real and personal property of intestates to the next of kin in equal degree ; and the power to devise and convey property of every kind. This was the first general legislation by the Congress of the United States on the subject of real property. It struck the key-note of our liberal system of land law, not only in the States formed out of the public domain, but also in the older States, and is the foundation of all the statutes of the United States relating to land tenures.[25]

The rest of the Ordinance proper related to the organization of a government, and directed how it should be administered. Congress was to appoint a governor for a term of three years, a secretary for four years, and three

---

23. The question of authorship brought into prominence by Webster, who, in his speech on Foote's resolution, ascribed the drafting of it to Nathan Dane. Upon the authorship see Peter Force, National Intelligencer, August 26, 1847. W. F. Poole : North American Review, No. 251, April, 1876. Hinsdale : *loc. cit.*, Chap. XV. Cutler : Life, Journals and Correspondence of Rev. Manassah Cutler. Vol. I., pp. 292-298, and Chap. VIII. Sato : *loc. cit.*, pp. 104-116.

24. Dunn : *loc. cit.*, p. 204.

25. Donaldson : *loc cit.*, pp. 156, 158 and 159.

judges to serve during good behavior. The governor was
to be commander-in-chief of the militia, appoint and commission militia officers below the rank of general officers,
and appoint such magistrates and other civil officers as he
deemed necessary for peace and good order. The secretary was to record territorial acts, and send copies of them
to Congress every six months. Any two of the judges
were to form a court having the common-law jurisdiction.
The governor and judges, acting together, were to
adopt such laws of the original States, civil and criminal,
as they deemed necessary and best suited to the circumstances of the district, which laws were to remain in force
unless disapproved of by Congress, until there should be
five thousand free male inhabitants, of full age. On at-
taining this population the district was to have a general assembly of its own, consisting of the governor, a
house of representatives, whose membership should be
in the proportion of one to every five hundred free
male inhabitants, and a legislative council of five, to be
chosen by Congress from a list of ten nominated by the
Territorial house of representatives. The representatives were to serve for two years, and the members of
council for five. The legislature thus constituted, was
given authority to make laws in all cases for the good
government of the district, not repugnant to the principles
and articles of this ordinance. No act was to have any force
without the assent of the governor, and he was given power
to convene, prorogue and dissolve the assembly when he
should think expedient. When a legislature should have
been formed, the council and house were to have authority to elect by joint ballot a delegate to Congress, who
should have a seat and a right to debate, but not to vote.
All the officers were required to reside in the Territory.
It was required that the governor should own a freehold
of one thousand acres of land in the district ; and that the
secretary, judges and members of council should own
similar freeholds of five hundred acres each. No one was
qualified to act as a representative, unless he had been a
citizen of one of the United States three years, and a resi-

dent in the district, or had resided in the district three years; and held in his own right two hundred acres of land within the same. The possession of a freehold of fifty acres in the district, and citizenship of one of the States, and residence in the district, or a like freehold and two years residence in the district, where the qualifications of the electors of representatives.

Then followed six "articles of compact between the original States and the people and States in the said territory," which were to "forever remain unalterable unless by common consent." The first provided that no peaceable or orderly person should "ever be molested on account of his mode of worship or religious sentiments." The second guaranteed to the inhabitants the benefits of the writ of *habeas corpus*, trial by jury, proportionate representation in the legislature, bail (except for capital offences) moderate fines and punishments, and the preservation of liberty and property. The article concluded with the declaration "that no law ought ever to be made or have force in the said territory that shall, in any manner whatever, interfere with or affect private contracts or engagements, *bona fide* and without fraud previously formed."[26] The third article declared that schools and means of education should forever be encouraged, and good faith should be observed toward the Indians. The fourth contained the articles of Jefferson's ordinance: That the territory and the States formed therein should forever remain a part of the confederacy, subject to the Articles of Confederation and to the authority of Congress under them; that they should be subject to pay a proportionate part of the Federal debts and expenses; should never interfere with the disposal of the soil by Congress, nor tax the lands of the United States or non-resident proprietors higher than resident. To this was added the provision that the navigation of the Mississippi and St. Lawrence should be free to every citizen of

---

26. This provision was copied into the Constitution of the United States a few weeks later, but this is its first appearance in our national legislation.

the United States "without any tax, impost or duty therefor."

Article V. provided for the formation in the territory of not less than three nor more than five States, and roughly indicated their boundaries very nearly as they are at present. Whenever any of these States should have sixty thousand free inhabitants, it was to be admitted "into the Congress of the United States on an equal footing with the original States, in all respects whatever," and was to be at liberty to form a permanent constitution and State government, republican in form and in conformity with these articles. The Sixth and last article declared that there should "be neither slavery nor involuntary servitude in the said territory, otherwise than in the punishment of crimes whereof the party shall have been duly convicted: provided always, That any person escaping into the same, from whom labor or service is lawfully claimed in any one of the original States, such fugitive may be lawfully reclaimed and conveyed to the person claiming his or her labor or service as aforesaid."

The " Power to Legislate " Embodied in the Constitution.

These two ordinances (of 1784 and of 1787) comprise the legislation relating to territorial government previous to the First Congress. But what right had the Congress of the Confederacy to establish a government for this territory ? or what right had the General Government, under the Articles of Confederation, to acquire territory at all ? These articles declared that the Congress had only such powers as were expressly delegated.[27] The power to acquire, the right to retain and the right to govern territory are nowhere in the articles, even by implication, granted to the United States.[28] And yet, "all this has been done, and done without the least color of constitutional author-

---

27. Article II.
28. Johnston: Lalor's Political Encyclopædia, Article on the Ordinance of 1787, III., p. 33.

ity. Yet no blame has been whispered, no alarm has been sounded."[29] The acquisition of this territory rested upon acts so directly and expressly connected with the establishment of the Confederation that the acquisition was itself one of the fundamental conditions of union. The declared purposes for which these acquisitions were made were that the lands should be disposed of for the common benefit, that the country should be settled and formed into republican States, and that these States should be admitted into the Union. In the cessions made and accepted upon these express conditions all of the States acquiesced. They may be said, therefore, to have conferred upon Congress an implied power to legislate to carry them into effect.[30]

Of the right of Congress to exercise this power, serious doubts were expressed at the time. So long as it was not to be found in the instrument under which the Congress was organized and its powers established, it was an authority liable to be doubted and denied. Thus it became eminently necessary to have it expressly stated and conferred in the instrument under which all the other functions of the government were to be exercised.[31]

In the plan of government presented by Governor Randolph at the opening of the Constitutional Convention of 1787, we find a resolution that provision ought to be made for the admission of new States, and in the first draft of the Constitution there was such a power contained. Madison at once proposed that additional powers be given " to dispose of the unappropriated lands of the United States ;" and "to institute temporary governments for new States arising therein." From these propositions there resulted the provisions that now stand in the third section of the fourth article of the Constitution:

"New States may be admitted by the Congress into this Union ; but no new State shall be formed or erected within the jurisdiction of any other State ; nor any State

---

29. Federalist, No. 38, January 15, 1788.
30. Curtis: Constitutional History of the United States, pp. 198, 536.
31. Curtis : *loc. cit.*, pp. 533 *et seq.*

be formed by the junction of two or more States; nor parts of States, without the consent of the legislatures of the States concerned as well as of the Congress.

"The Congress shall have power to dispose of and make all needful rules and regulations respecting the Territory or other property belonging to the United States; and nothing in this Constitution shall be so construed as to prejudice any claims of the United States, or of any particular State."

It was, then, with this constitutional authority that the First Congress in 1789, took up the question of the government of the Northwest Territory, and promptly re-enacted the Ordinance of 1787, making such changes as were necessary to adapt the Ordinance to the new Constitution [32]

II.

With the authority specifically vested by the fourth article of the Constitution, and with the powers by implication from the right to acquire territory, Congress has organized Territories, and made laws for their government, on a scale which was never anticipated. There have been in all twenty-eight Territories organized,[1] and from the establishment of a government for "the Northwest," down to the present day there has never been a time when Congress has not had one or more organized Territories under its control, so that the legislation for their government has beeen practically unbroken.[2] It is the object of this paper to trace the changes that have taken place in this legislation : to show that the Territorial government as it exists to-day, however greatly it may differ from that first established for the Northwest, is yet a direct development from the Ordinance of 1787, and that the process of development has been as gradual as it has been unceasing.

---

32. See Appendix B. 1), also *supra*, p. 3.
1. See Appendix A.   2. See Appendix B.

The legislation of Congress with regard to the government of the Territories, divides of itself into two periods. For thirty years the Ordinance of 1787 was the model in establishing the governments in the Territories. The usual method of Congress was to carve out a portion of the public domain, and establish a Territory by name, re-enacting, with slight additions, an existing law relating to some other Territory, so that the Ordinance of 1787, in terms or effect, with slight modifications, was extended over or embraced in the organic laws and acts for all the Territories of the Union. Even as late as 1849 the Ordinance of 1787 is specifically referred to.[3] A second period begins in 1836 with the organic act for the Territory of Wisconsin. All of the organic acts for the sixteen Territories established since that time are modeled directly upon that. But the Wisconsin act is not in itself an innovation. It marks the beginning of a new period, only because it defines the powers and duties of a Territory and its people for the first time in the form which has since been universally followed. The statement in Donaldson's Public Domain (p. 418), that the Florida act of 1822 "was really the first organic act" is quite mistaken, for the Florida act is an almost literal copy of the act for Orleans of 1804 ; and Professor Johnston's statement[4] that the form of government established by the Orleans act of 1804, " was the model regularly followed afterward," is equally misleading. All of the main features that Professor Johnston enumerates, including the modifications made for Missouri in the act of 1812, are to be found in the Ordinance of 1787. It is the form of the Orleans enactment that makes it important. It is the first breaking away from the Ordinance of 1787, which even then was being vested with the halo which now crowns it. It contains merely the germ, however, but nothing more, of the form of the Wisconsin act, and does not mark the beginning of the

---

3. In the organic act for Minnesota.
4. Lalor's Political Encyclopædia, Article, Territories, p. 919.

new period, for it was not until 1836 that this new form of enactment was universally accepted.[5]

FIRST PERIOD. 1789-1835.

Though the Ordinance of 1787 was enacted solely for the territory northwest of the Ohio it was evidently intended, or at any rate eminently fitted so general were its provisions, to be applied to the territory south of that river as well, and the acts of cession by North Carolina[6] and Georgia[7] stipulated that such should be the case. Accordingly for all the southern Territories the governments that were established were regulated by the provisions of the Ordinance. But with the acquisition of the Louisiana country beyond the Mississippi, and so outside of the original limits of the United States, a new element entered in. Congress had to deal with a country that was not considered in the making of the Ordinance and with a people whose previous training had not fitted them for the freedom and responsibility which the government under the Ordinance entailed. Consequently, for a few years, so much of its time as Congress gave to the consideration of the Territories was occupied almost exclusively with the Territories west of the Mississippi. When this question had been more or less satisfactorily settled, there followed a period in which the Territorial institutions were made to conform to the democratic spirit that was spreading throughout the country, as manifested by the placing in the hands of the people more and more power in the control of the government. Then came the second acquiring of territory beyond the original limits, and while, as will be seen, this democratic tendency did not cease, for our purpose, it is more important, from the time of the acquisition of the Floridas to trace the combination of tendencies and enactments which was leading to the second period in our Territorial legislation.

---

5. Michigan, 1805 ; Illinois, 1809 ; and Alabama, 1817, all organized after 1804 and according to the Ordinance.

6. See p. 16.   7. See p. 17.

We thus find that again the first period falls into four divisions :

1.) Territories east of the Mississippi.
2.) Territories west of the Mississippi.
3.) Until the organization of the Territory of Florida.
4.) From the organization of Florida to the end of the First Period.

1.) Territories East of the Mississippi.

Within a year after the First Congress had re-enacted the Ordinance of 1787 the cession of her Western lands by North Carolina had been made[8] and accepted,[9] and a Territory out of them had been organized.[10] In accordance with the terms of the deed of cession,[11] Congress established a government in all respects similar to that of the Northwest Territory, as set forth in the Ordinance, except that the provisions of the sixth article prohibiting slavery were not to be in force. This Territory, which was designated as the Territory South of the river Ohio, was the first to organize a legislature.[12]

As soon as this first Territorial legislature was formed, as provided by the Ordinance, they elected a delegate to Congress.[13] Considerable debate arose in the House, when his credentials were presented to that body, upon the propriety of admitting such a "nondescript" member,[14] but he was finally given a seat, with the right of debating but not of voting. The privilege of franking was extended to him, and there was allowed him the same compensation

---

8. February 25, 1790.   9. April 2, 1790.

10. May 26, 1790. See appendix B 4).

11. There were ten conditions in North Carolina's act of cession, of which the only one of importance for us was the fourth : that there should be a government established in all respects similar to that of the Northwest Territory according to the Ordinance : *"Provided always,* That no regulations made or to be made by Congress shall tend to emancipate slaves."

12. August 25, 1794.

13. September 3, 1794.

14. Benton : Abridg. Debates of Congress, Vol. I., p. 530.

for traveling expenses and attendance in Congress as to the members of the House.[15] The same rights, privileges, and compensation were granted in 1800 to the first delegate from the Northwest Territory,[16] and two years later the same provisions were made for any delegate to Congress who should be admitted to a seat.[17] As he was not given a vote the powers of a delegate were greatly restricted, but the advantage to a Territory of having such an agent in Congress was very great, for through him they could bring their affairs before that body in a manner which necessitated recognition.[18] The people of the Territories appreciated this and recognized the importance of the office to them. As they were required by the Ordinance to have organized a legislature before they could send a delegate, they advanced as their strongest argument for being permitted to organize, or for proceeding to organize a legislature, that they would then be allowed to have an agent in Congress. And this was one of the first offices that they requested should be made, and the first that was made elective by the people.[19]

Until the organization of a legislature, the governor and judges in the Territories were to exercise the legislative function, but they were only empowered to adopt suitable laws taken from the statute books of the original States. That this was not as much of a restriction as one would at first suppose may be gathered from the adoption

---

15. December 3, 1794.   16. See Appendix B. 8) and 11).

17. Appendix B. 14)

18. Wm. Henry Harrison, delegate from Northwest Territory, in 1800, "Secured the passage of a bill (revising the method of land sales) which in time did far more for the good of his country, than his great victory over the Prophet at Tippecanoe, or his defeat of Tecumseh at the battle of the Thames."—McMaster: History of People of United States. Vol. II., p. 481. See also Burnet: Notes on the North-west, p. 302. Dunn: *loc. cit.*, p. 283.

19. By Ordinance members of lower house of Territorial legislature were elective, this the first office made elective after that. First elective in Mississippi in 1808. By 1819 elective in all the Territories. Since 1817 delegates have been elected every second year for the same term as members of House.

by the governor and judges of the Northwest Territory of an old Virginia statute of the colonial period, by which "the common law of England, and all general statutes in aid of the common law prior to the fourth year of James I" were put in force in the Territory. But in spite of the wide range that was open to them the provision was found to be inconvenient. Not only were many of the laws not adapted to be thus thrust upon a community that was not considered in the making of them, but special circumstances required special legislation. Accordingly to meet the requirements of the case the governor and judges thought it necessary to overstep their authority and enact laws. And this practice was not formally disapproved by Congress, but was even tolerated and accepted. [20]

It was undoubtedly in a large part to obviate this difficulty that the first change in the principles of the Ordinance was made. This was that the provisions relating to the organization of a general assembly were not to depend upon the size of the population but were to be in force as soon as satisfactory evidence should be given to the governor that it was the wish of the majority of the freeholders. It was first enacted in 1800 when the Northwest

---

20. May 8, 1792, Congress enacted, " That the laws of the Territory Northwest of the river Ohio, that have been or hereafter may be enacted by the governor and judges . . . ." and, " That the governor and judges are authorized to repeal the laws by them made."

In 1794, the laws of the Northwest Territory passed from July to December, 1792, were referred to a special committee of the House, who reported that, with one exception, they ought to be disapproved, as the governor and judges had exceeded their authority in passing them. A resolution to that effect was agreed to by the House, but in the Senate, on the report of a special committee, it was disagreed to.

Report of House Committee, February 19, 1801 : " . . . . .and from time to time, till the second grade of government was established, the Legislature enacted laws not derived from the codes of the States." Amer. State Papers : Miscellaneous, I. pp. 83, 283. See also Hinsdale : *loc. cit.*, p. 298. Burnet : *loc. cit.*, pp. 39, 63, 04 and 312, *cf.* further, p. 21 for District of Louisiana.

Territory was divided and the Territory of Indiana established with a government according to the Ordinance. [21]

That part of the Territory south of the river Ohio that had been ceded by the State of North Carolina was organized as the State of Tennessee and was admitted into the Union in 1796. [22] This left unorganized the cession of South Carolina, which was now known as "the Territory of the United States south of the State of Tennessee." April 7, 1798, Congress accepted the cession of Georgia and adding it to the South Carolina cession organized the whole as the Territory of Mississipi. The government that was established was exactly the same as that which had been set up in the Territory South of the Ohio.[23] That is, it was according to the Ordinance except for the provisions prohibiting slavery. At the same time the importation of slaves into the Territory from without the limits of the United States was forbidden. In 1800 a further act was passed for settling the limits of the Territory, [24] and the provisions that had just been adopted for the Territory of Indiana were extended to Mississippi also, that is, the organization of a general assembly was not to depend upon the number of inhabitants but upon the wish of the majority of the freeholders. It was further enacted that the general assembly of Mississippi should meet at least once each year.

2.) Territories West of the Mississippi.

The United States acquired the Province of Louisiana from France in 1803. As soon as the treaty ceding the country was ratified, Congress authorized[25] the President to take possession of and occupy the Territories, and until further provision should be made for the government, all the military, civil, and judicial powers exercised by the officers of the existing government were to be vested in such persons as the President should appoint "for main-

---

21. May 7, 1800.   See Appendix B. 9).   22. See Appendix A
23. Appendix B. 7).   24. Appendix B. 10).
25. Appendix B. 17), 18) and 19).

tainiug and protecting the inhabitants in the free enjoyment of their liberty, property and religion." Accordingly the President vested the powers exercised by the governor and intendant of Louisiana in Governor Claiborne, of the Mississippi Territory, who assumed the government in December, but before the expiration of the session Congress had passed, an act establishing Territorial governments in the country.[26]

By this act the country ceded by France was divided into two parts, and all North of the 33d parallel of north latitude was formed into a district, to be known as the District of Louisiana. Its government was to be administered by the governor, secretary, and judges of the Indiana Territory, whose respective powers were extended over the District. This practically amounted to attaching the District to the Territory of Indiana for judicial and administrative purposes. But the governor and judges were authorized to *make* all laws that they might deem conducive to good government in this new District,[27] and it was specified that this included the power to establish inferior courts and prescribe their jurisdiction and duties. There were also further provisions, that the laws should be consistent with the Constitution and laws of the United States, that they should not interfere with the free exercise of religion, and that trial by jury should always be allowed.[28]

All south of the 33d parallel was organized as the Territory of Orleans. The executive power was vested in a governor, and in a secretary, from neither of whom property qualifications were required, their powers, however, were the same as those granted by the Ordinance, except that the governor had the additional power to grant pardons for offences against the Territory, and reprieves for those against the United States until the decision of the President should be made known. The legislative powers were vested in the governor and a

26. March 26, 1804.
27. *Cf.* p. 19.   28. See further, Appendix B. 20).

council of thirteen, appointed annually by the President, from among the property holders who had resided in the Territory one year and held no office of profit under the Territory or United States. The members of council were to be paid $4 per day during their attendance at sessions[29]. In both the Territory of Orleans and the District of Louisiana the laws were to be reported to Congress, and if disapproved of were to be of no force. As in the Ordinance, there was a superior court which consisted of three judges appointed by the President, but they as well as the justices of the peace were to hold office only for four years. A United States district court distinct from the Superior Court of the Territory was also established, with four sessions annually at Orleans, the judge of which was given the same jurisdiction and powers as the judge of the United States Kentucky district[30].

It was further provided that the judges of the superior court were to have jurisdiction in all criminal cases, and exclusive jurisdiction in all those which were capital ; and original and appellate jurisdiction in all civil cases of the value of $100. The ordinance of 1787 had simply stated that there was to be a court of three judges, any two of whom were to form a court, who were to have a common-law jurisdiction. Though the power had not been delegated we find the Territorial legislatures had assumed by a sort of common consent the power to regulate the courts and their jurisdiction, as well as to fix the times and places of holding court. [31] These specifications concern-

---

29. This, the first instance of the United States paying the members of a Territorial legislature. It was in force only one year, and does not occur again until the organization of Florida.

30. This the only instance of a Federal district court being permanently established in any Territory. By the judiciary act of 1801, Appendix B. 12), the Territories of Ohio and Indiana constituted one of the four districts of the sixth circuit, but this act was repealed a year later and the old order restored. See acts of March 3, 1805, and April 18, 1806, p. 25. An attorney and a marshal were appointed for Orleans. *Cf.* p. 29 and Appendix B. 49). See further Clinton *vs.* Englebrecht, 13, Wall, 434.

31. *Cf.* p. 21.

ing the judiciary which are to be found for the first time in the Federal Statutes in this act for Orleans were the result of experience in the other Territories, [32] and these same provisions enlarged and developed we will find hereafter incorporated in the organic acts of all the new Territories as formed. [33]

It is to be noted that by this act full legislative powers in both of the Territories were given to officers in the choosing of whom the people had no voice The citizens of Louisiana were accustomed to the arbitrary methods of the Spanish and French officers in the Province, and were therefore scarcely fitted to assume the responsibilities of self-government, and a certain amount of training was undoubtedly needed to prepare them for the duties of citizenship.[34] But legislation without representation was so utterly at variance with all principles of government prevalent throughout the United States that the provisions we have spoken of could not pass unchallenged. In the District of Louisiana it did not make so much difference. There it was only conferring expressly a power which had previously been assumed by the governor and judges in all of the Territories. [35] But its enactment even under such circumstances marks a very distinct step. With the Territory of Orleans the case was altogether different. The population was much greater than in the District of Louisiana. So numerous in fact as to warrant the demand that they made to be admitted as a State into the Union.[36] Were not the provisions of this act inconsistent with the articles of the treaty, which stipulated that "the inhabitants should be admitted as soon as possible to the enjoyment of all the rights, advantages, and immunities of citizens of the United States?" It was the Senate that had insisted upon this obnoxious feature, to which the more

32. Reports of House Committees, 21st Congress, 1st session, No. 304.

33. For further provisions for Territory of Orleans, see Appendix B. 20).

34 Carr : Missouri, pp. 86 and 87.   35. See p. 19. *supra.*

36. Journals of Congress, Dec. 31. 1804.

democratic House of Representatives had strenuously objected. The latter were finally persuaded to consent, but only on condition that the act should not remain in force for more than one year.

At the expiration of the year such a storm of protest had been aroused that Congress was glad to make very radical changes. Only such of its provisions were continued in force as did not conflict with the two acts then passed, one for the Territory of Orleans, [37] the other for the District of Louisiana, which was now changed into a Territory of the same name. [38] In the former a government in all respect similar to that exercised in Mississippi was established, except : at the first election there were to be twenty-five representatives chosen ; the governor, secretary and judges were to receive the salaries granted by the act of 1804 ; [39] and the second paragraph of the Ordinance of 1787 which regulates the descent and distribution of estates was excluded from operation. [40] The act for the Territory of Louisiana simply re-established the government of the year before, but gave the Territory officers of its own instead of entrusting their duties to the Indiana officials. The powers and duties of the governor and secretary were defined, but, as in Orleans, no property qualifications were required and the governor was empowered to grant pardons and reprieves. The judges and other officers were given the same jurisdiction and powers and compensation as by law established for similar offices in Indiana. [41] The act is thus a combination of the Ordinance of 1787 and the Orleans act of 1804. The government established is according to the Ordinance but the form of enactment is like that of Orleans.

As has been stated, the attention of Congress during these few years was occupied almost exclusively with the Territories west of the Mississippi. There were however three important acts passed relating to the other Terri-

---

37. March 2, 1805.   38. March 3, 1805.
39. See Appendix B. 20).   40. See further Appendix B. 25).
41. See further Appendix B. 26).

tories. On January 11, 1805, the Territory of Michigan was cut off from Indiana with a government exactly the same as that administered in Indiana. [42] On March 3rd, of the same year, the superior courts of all the Territories in which Federal district courts had not been established [43] were given the same jurisdiction and powers as exercised by the district court of the Kentucky district ; and writs of error and appeals were to lie to the Supreme Court of the United States just as from the Kentucky district court. [44] And April 18, 1806, the provisions of the act of February 28, 1799, which provided for the compensation of jurors, attorneys, etc., were extended to the Territories so far as they may relate to this act of 1805.

3.) Until the Organization of the Territory of Florida.

From the time of the establishment of a Territorial government in the Northwest Congress had been in receipt of petitions from the people, resolutions of societies, and memorials by the legislatures, praying for the extension of the suffrage. Delegate after delegate from each of the Territories had introduced resolutions and motions to that effect, and had asked for the appointment of committees to consider the question. [45] In the House committees had been appointed and had even reported favorably, [46] but no action had been taken [47] until on January 9, 1808, for the Mississippi Territory the delegate to Congress was made elective by the electors of the lower

42. See further Appendix B. 24).

43. That is in all of the Territories except Orleans.

44. *Cf.* American State Papers. Miscellaneous I. pp 116 and 117. II. 384 and 385.

45. Annals of Congress, December 14, 1802. February 8, 1803, January 4, 1805.

46. Annals of Congress, February 9, 1805, February 14, 1806.

47. In 1807 the House passed a bill, one section of which extended the right of suffrage to the citizens of the Mississippi Territory, but this part of the bill was struck out in the Senate.

house of the Territorial legislature, [48] and the suffrage was given to all free white males of age, who were citizens of the United States and residents in the Territory one year preceding the election, and who had legal or equitable title to a tract of land from the United States of fifty acres, or who owned town lot of the value of $100.[49] From this time on the right of suffrage and the number of offices that were made elective were rapidly extended. February 26, 1808, in Indiana, the qualifications for suffrage were made the same as in Mississippi. One year later the delegate in Indiana was made elective and the electors of the lower house were also authorized to elect their members of council. [50] In 1811 the suffrage in Indiana was further extended to every free white male of age, who had paid a county or Territorial tax, and had resided in the Territory one year previous to any general election, and was a resident at the time of the election.[51] The Territory of Illinois was cut off from Indiana in 1809, [52] and in 1812 when it was authorized to organize a legislature the suffrage qualifications and the offices elective were made the same as in Indiana. [53] The Territory of Missouri was organized in 1812, [54] and the question arose in Congress as to the advisability of requiring voters to be freeholders. Randolph, of Virginia, held for property qualifications and quoted the practice in his State. Maryland was at once cited as an example of a State that had tried it and given it up. When it was finally decided to make the suffrage qualifications the same as in Indiana, this principle may be regarded as established, for two years later the same provisions were put in force in Mississippi. [55]

To speak, as has just been done of the organization

---

48. See p. 18.   49. For further provisions of this and following acts, see Appendix B. under respective dates.

50. February 27, 1809,   51. March 3, 1811.

52. February 3, 1809.   53. May 20, 1812.   54. June 4, 1812.

55. October 25, 1814. Michigan the only other Territory then organized, (See Appendix A.) and had then no elective officers as it had not yet formed a legislature.

of Missouri in 1812 is scarcely correct, for it was not a
new Territory that was organized but an old one reorganized. Orleans was organized as the State of Louisiana,
and the Territory which had borne the latter name was
changed into the Territory of Missouri. With the change
in name a new act was passed, in reality merely permitting the Territory of Louisiana to proceed to organize
a legislature, but of importance because it set forth in
greater detail than had ever been done before the powers
and duties of the various officers, and thus marks a distinct
step towards our Second Period. Further, the right of
the governor to prorogue the general assembly was taken
away, though he was still permitted to exercise an absolute
veto upon their legislative acts and he retained the power
to convene them on extraordinary occasions. There had
been many complaints previously in the Territories, that
the powers of the governor were too great, and Congress
had often considered the advisability of restricting them,
but nothing had ever come of it before.[56] The provisions
regarding the general assembly were taken from the
Ordinance, except that the number of members and their
qualifications for office were slightly different, and it was
specified that the legislature had power to establish and
regulate inferior courts and justices of the peace and other
civil offices, and it was ordered that the sessions should be
annual. As in the Orleans act of 1804 the superior judges
were to be appointed for four years only, and the jurisdiction and powers which we there noted as having been
given to them as the result of experience [57] we find incorporated in this act. The presence of two judges also was
required to hold a court, as the practice of allowing one
to do so had proven unwise [58] Sections 14 and 15 of this

56. See Journals of Congress, February 17, April 12, November
18, 1808, and January 20, 1812. Burnet : *loc. cit.*, p. 306. Hinsdale :
loc. cit., p. 305.

57. P. 23, N. 32, *supra.* and Amer. State Papers : Misc. vol. II.
p. 373. Burnet : *loc. cit.*, pp. 62 and 63.

58. By the Ordinance two judges were required to hold a court.
Owing to the extent of Territory and the amount of business

act, the one a bill of rights and the other placing certain restrictions on the legislative power, were taken directly from the Ordinance. [59]

During the next ten years (1812-1821) aside from the fact that two new Territories were organized, Alabama in 1817 [60] and Arkansas in 1819, [61] two features in the enactments of Congress relating to the Territories are worthy of especial note : a) The putting in force in other Territories provisions which the experience of one had proven wise ; and b) The systematizing of the judiciary.

a) *Legislation as the result of experience.*

That the specifications concerning the judiciary in the Orleans Act of 1804, and the requiring in Missouri of the presence of two judges to hold court, were the result of experience, we have already noticed. [62] We have also seen how the extension of the suffrage passed from one Territory to another. [63] The legislation to which attention is now called is but a further carrying out of the same policy. The Delegate to Congress made elective first in Mississippi, and then in Indiana and Illinois [64] was made elective in all the Territories "every second year for the same term of two years that the members of the House " were elected for. [65] The number of the members of council in Mississippi was made the same as in Missouri. [66] The members of council elective in Indiana and Illinois [67] were made

---

before them it was thought advisable to permit one judge to do so. It was so ordered by act of May 8, 1792. An appeal lay to the superior court from the inferior courts, in which the presence of two judges was required. So a suitor was forced to appeal from the decision of two men to that of one. It would sometimes happen that the superior court would be presided over by one judge at one term, and by the other two judges at the next. Hence the same point of law would often be decided upon differently, and great confusion would in consequence arise. *Cf.* also Appendix B. 38).

59. For further provisions see Appendix B. 45).
60. Appendix B. 59) and 61).   61. Appendix B. 67) and 70).
62. See pp. 23 and 27 *supra*.   63. See pp. 25 and 26 *supra*.
64. See p. 26, *supra*.   65. March 3, 1817.
66. Appendix B. 45) and 52).   67. See p. 26 *supra*.

elective also in Missouri. [68] The presence of two judges was required in Indiana to hold court. [69] District and Territorial judges were required to reside within their respective districts and Territories. [70] And an attorney and a marshal for the United States were to be appointed in every Territory. [71] The same feature of policy will be at once seen in considering the enactment for the judiciary during this decade.

b) The systematization of the Territorial judiciary.

In 1815 an act was passed for Illinois [72] by which the Territory was divided into three circuits and the superior judges were to hold courts in each with jurisdiction in all cases over $20 ; the three judges together were to form a court of appeals with appellate jurisdiction over these circuit courts and all inferior courts, but no question of appeal could be decided without the concurrence of two judges. The following year [73] it was enacted that this law should only remain in force until the end of the next session of the Territorial legislature, and that then that legislature should have power itself to organize the courts. But on the very same day the general assembly of Missouri was ordered to establish a system of circuit and appellate courts similar to that of Illinois [74] In Missouri and also in Indiana the superior judges were given chancery powers in all civil cases. [75] When the Territory of Alabama was cut off from Mississippi and Arkansas from Missouri [76] in each case the judiciary was organized on the principles just outlined : each of the superior judges held courts in the several counties with general jurisdiction, and from these there lay an appeal to the superior court, which also had exclusive jurisdiction given to the Territorial superior courts by the act of 1805. In 1818 the jurisdiction of the general court of Alabama was extended to all cases of admiralty and maritime jurisdiction,

---

68. April 29, 1816. 69. Appendix B. 54).
70. Appendix B. 48). 71. See p. 22 N. 30 and Appendix B. 49).
72. March 3, 1815. 73. April 29, 1 816. 74. Appendix B. 58)
75. April 29, 1816. 76. See p. 28.

subject to appeals to the Supreme Court of the United States, as allowed in similar cases from the United States circuit courts. [77]

4.) From the Organization of Florida to the End of the First Period.

The treaty with Spain, by which the United States acquired the Floridas was concluded February 22, 1819, and the ratifications were exchanged exactly two years later. [78] For protecting "the inhabitants in the free enjoyment of their liberty, property, and religion," the same course was pursued as previously in Louisiana. Until the organization of a government, the President was authorized to take possession of the country, and to vest the powers of the existing goverment in such persons as he thought best, [79] and the President appointed Major General Andrew Jackson governor of the Floridas, and vested in him all the powers of the Captain General, Intendant, and Governors. In 1822 Congress established a Territorial government in the Floridas, [80] modeled directly on that first established for Orleans, and indeed the act for Florida was in most parts copied word for word from the act of 1804. The striking feature of the Orleans government it will be remembered was a legislative council in the choice of which the people had no voice. [81] The legislative council of Florida was to be composed in the same way, though the members were not required to be property holders ; the governor was not given power to convene and prorogue them, and the sessions were limited to one each year, and to four weeks in length. There was no district court established as in Orleans, [82] but there were two superior courts of one judge each, with jurisdiction similar to the other Territorial superior courts. The

---

77. Appendix B. 64).
78. See Appendix B. 72).
79. See Appendix B. 68) and 73) and *cf.* 39).
80. March 30, 1822.   81. See pp. 23 *et seq. supra.*
82. See p. 22, and N. 30.

Territory was entitled to a delegate in Congress and for his election for the first time in the history of our Territories the qualifications for the exercise of the suffrage, were left to the legislature to determine. [83]

The next year this act was modified in several particulars. [84] A previous residence of six months was required of the members of council and of twelve months of the delegate to Congress. By a two-thirds vote the council was enabled to pass a bill over the governor's veto. All bills to tax the inhabitants or their property were required to have the consent of Congress before they became laws, [85] and writs of error and appeals from the superior courts to the United States Supreme Court were allowed in the same manner as from the circuit courts of the United States, where the amount in controversy exceeded $1,000.

To appreciate the significance of the legislation of these closing years of the First Period it must be borne in mind that there were but three Territories in existence—Michigan, Arkansas and Florida. In Florida the form of government was that first established in Orleans in 1804, a form justified on the ground that the people were not fitted to assume the responsibilities of self-government. [86] In Arkansas, which was a part of the Louisiana country, we have traced the advance from similar beginnings of non-representative government through the first stage of government of the Ordinance of 1787 to a modified form of the second stage according to that Ordinance—whereby both houses of the legislature were elective by the people, property qualifications were not required for the exercise of the suffrage, and a systematized judiciary was established. [87] In Michigan although the Territory had been organized in 1805 there still remained the primitive form of government that had been first established for the North

---

83. For further provisions see Appendix B. 74).
84. March 3, 1823.
85. *Cf*. Appendix B. 75). Repealed April 28, 1828.
86. See p. 23.
87. See pp. 21, 24, 26-28, and Appendix B. 67).

west Territory by the Ordinance of 1787, that is, there
was no legislature, only a governor and three judges with
power to adopt laws from the original States. The population of the Territory had increased sufficiently to warrant
the organization of a legislature, but when the question
was submitted to the people in 1818, it was answered by a
decided negative. The most of the people were French,
the duties and burdens of self-government seemed to have
no attractions for them, they found no reason to complain
of the existing state of affairs, and so cared for no
change.[88] The following year, however, they were given
the privilege of electing a delegate to Congress.[89]

The governments of these three Territories thus
differed widely from each other. The policy of Congress
which we noticed as being characteristic of the third
division of this Period, viz: the putting in force in other
Territories provisions which the experience of one had
proven wise, is still more noticeable in the present
division, and it goes one step further in that the legislation
shows a very marked tendency towards the establishment
of a uniform system of Territorial government.

In 1823,[90] the Governor of Michigan, as in the other
Territories that had been recently organized, was given
power to grant pardons for offences against the Territory
and reprieves for those against the United States. The
same powers as those of the general assembly under the
Ordinance were vested in a council of nine, who were to
serve for a term of two years and were to be appointed
by the President from eighteen persons to be chosen by
the electors of the delegate to Congress. The members
were to be paid for mileage and attendance, the sessions
in any one year were not to exceed sixty days, and no law
was to be valid after it had been disapproved by Congress.
The Superior judges were given chancery as well as
common-law jurisdiction and their terms were limited to
four years.

---

88. Cooley : Michigan, p. 198.   89. Appendix B. 65).
90. March 3, 1823. See Appendix B.

When in 1824 an additional superior court was established in Florida—making three in all—the opportunity
was seized to organize the judiciary upon a system similar
to that of Arkansas : A system of superior courts with
general jurisdiction, the judges of which together formed
a court of appeals. From this appellate court writs of error
and appeal were allowed to the Supreme Court of the
United States as from the circuit courts, where the amount
in controversy was over $1,000. [91] In 1826 these pro-
visions were again changed, but the changes consisted
chiefly in granting an increase in jurisdiction to the three
superior courts. [92] They were given admiralty and maritime jurisdiction, and cognizance of all cases under
Federal laws, with power to grant new trials, where there
had been trials by jury, for the reasons for which new trials
had usually been granted by courts of law. By this same
act of 1826 the legislative council was made elective, and
a previous residence of one year was required of the
members. Members of council were declared ineligible
to any office created during the period of their service,
or the fees of which had been regulated while they were
members, or for one year thereafter. [93]

The right of appeal from the highest court of the
Territory to the Supreme Court of the United States was

---

91. See Appendix B. 81).　　92. See Appendix B. 77).

93. By the Orleans act of 1804 the members of council were to
be paid $4 per day during attendance. Similarly in the first act for
Florida the members of council were to be paid $3 per day and $3
for every twenty miles in going to and returning from each session.
This privilege had been greatly abused. For a distance of two or
three hundred miles, some of the members had charged ten, some
twelve, and some thirteen hundred and fifty miles travel. Congress
learned of this and in the act we are now considering inserted a
clause that mileage should only be paid for every twenty miles,
"estimated by the actual distance from the place of residence to the
seat of government, and so distinctly certified by the governor."
In 1828 a similar restrictive clause was enacted for Arkansas, and
from that time on in modified form it is to be found in the organic
act of each Territory. Since the organization of Wisconsin, 1836, it
had been worded "by the nearest actually traveled route."

granted in Michigan in 1825,[94] as it had previously been granted in Florida, when two years later[95] in the same Territory the people were authorized to elect their members of council the same restriction was enacted that had been passed for Florida, that no member of council should be eligible for any office that was created or the fees of which were regulated during his period of service and for one year after. The members of the legislature of Arkansas were granted in 1828[96] mileage and payment for attendance, and at the same time it was ordered that the sessions should be biennial and limited to thirty days.

It has already been stated (p. 16) that, while the most important features of the legislation of the closing years of the First Period was the tendency to establish a uniform system of Territorial government, the democratic element was not wanting. This has been clearly evidenced in the enactments that have given, especially in those for Michigan and Florida. Still further, in Michigan in 1825, the qualified electors in each county were permitted to elect all their township and county officers, with the exception of the judicial officers; and the same privilage was granted to Florida and Arkansas in 1829.[97] The last act to be considered forms a fitting close to a period that has witnessed the steady placing in the hands of the people more and more power in the control of the government. It was enacted for Arkansas in 1832 and ordered that every free white male citizen, twenty-one years of age, who had resided in the Territory six months preceding, should be given the privilage of voting for all elective officers of the Territory.

Much of the legislation that has been enumerated is a striking and continuous proof of the evident losing of faith in the efficacy of general principles.[98] The Ordinance of 1787 was passed in the formative period of our

94. February 5, 1825.   95. January 29, 1827.

96. Appendix B. 96), and p. 33 N. 93.

97. In Arkansas legislature authorized to overrule Governor's veto by ⅔ vote. See further Appendix B. 97).

98. Cf. Bryce : The American Commonwealth, I. p. 456.

institutions, a period that is marked by the wide-spread interest in theories of government, and the Ordinance stands almost on a par with our Constitution for the simplicity and universality of its provisions. But it did not take Congress very long to learn that if they wished to have a thing done in a manner which they considered good, it was just as well to do it themselves. It was impossible for Congress to enter into all the details of Territorial government but we have seen how more and more Congress specified the way in which the government should be administered. The enactments regarding the judiciary are an excellent example of this. They form the greatest part of the legislation that we have considered, yet they only make three additions to the principles of the Ordinance: that the superior courts of the Territories should have jurisdiction in cases in which the United States were a party; that there should be appeals from the Territorial superior courts to the Federal Supreme Court; and that the judges should exercise chancery powers as well as common-law jurisdiction.

The extension of the suffrage and the increase in the number of elective offices have been so fully brought out in detailing the enactments that further reference to them here is unnecessary, but the ever increasing inclination of Congress to assume absolute control of the Territories should be noticed. It is best evidenced by the interference of Congress in the working of the legislatures. The payment of their expenses from the Federal treasury was the first decisive step in this direction.[99] The restrictions on the length and frequency of the sessions followed as a natural consequence, and soon Congress stepped in to prohibit certain kinds of legislation which had formerly been considered the undoubted right of local governing bodies. This was to go on undisputed until the question of the prohibition of slavery in the Territories arose, the solution of which established the absolute legislative authority of Congress over the Territories.

99. See p. 22, N. 29.

As a result of the confused and somewhat experimental legislation of the forty-five years of the First Period, the following changes in the form of Territorial government under the Ordinance have become established:

1). Congress has the right to divide any Territory or change its boundaries as it chooses.[100]

2). The governor cannot prorogue the legislature.

3). The governor may grant pardons for offenses against the Territory and reprieves for those against the United States, until the decision of the President be made known.

4). The legislature and 5), the Delegate to Congress shall be elected by the people

6). All local officers are to be elected by the people or they are left to the legislature to determine.

7). Property qualifications for the exercise of the suffrage have been abolished.

8). Every voter is eligible to every office.

9). Expenses of the legislature are paid by the United States.

10). The sessions of the legislature are limited in length and frequency.

11). The members of the legislature shall not be eligible during their term or for one year thereafter to any office which has been created or the emoluments of which have been increased during that time.

12). There shall be an organized judiciary consisting of a superior court, district courts, and other inferior courts.

13). The superior court must be held by a quorum of the superior judges, while each of the district courts may be held by one of the superior judges.

14). The legislature may be authorized to fix the jurisdiction of all the courts, always provided:

---

100. See Appendix B. 23), 25), 42), 63), 82), 110), and cf. 47).

a). That justices of the peace do not have jurisdiction in land questions, or where the amount in controversy exceeds a certain fixed sum (commonly $100).

b). That the supreme and district courts have chancery as well as common-law jurisdiction.

c). That writs of error and appeal lie from the district courts to the Territorial supreme court and from that court to the Supreme Court of the United States where the amount in controversy exceeds $1,000. And

d). That the district courts in all cases arising under the laws and Constitution of the United States have the same jurisdiction as is vested in the United States circuit and district courts, with appeal to the Territorial supreme court as in other cases.

15). An attorney and a marshal for the United States are appointed in every Territory.

16). The legislature is authorized to locate the seat of government of the Territory. [101]

Two other very important changes should be noted that have been introduced but cannot yet be regarded as established for they are not to be found in the organic acts of the Territories that were next organized. They are:

1). The enabling the legislature by a two-thirds vote to overrule the governor's veto ; and

2). The shortening of the term of the superior judges to four years.

---

101. See Appendix B. 9), 10), 24), 35), 61), 67), 74), 77), *cf*. 97).

When Congress in 1800 removed the seat of government of Northwest Territory to Chillicothe it was considered in that territory as a manifest usurpation of authority. Burnet : *loc. cit.* p 316.

III.

SECOND PERIOD 1836--1895.

The Second Period in the legislation of Congress for the Territories begins with the establishment of the Territory of Wisconsin in 1836. During the First Period there were differences in the forms of enactment, which organized the various Territorial governments, and there were differences in the forms of government that were established. It was a period of experiment. But when Congress came to organize the Territory of Wisconsin there was no longer any question. The government that was established was based upon the Ordinance of 1787 with the changes which we have seen emerging from the detailed legislation of the First Period. It was the first time that these changes were comprehended in one enactment, but so thoroughly had the work of Congress been done, so firmly had these principles become established that the organic acts of the sixteen Territories that have since been established are but copies of the Wisconsin Act of 1836.[1] Changes and modifications there were, as we shall see, but they were so slight as to be of comparatively little importance.

Such a uniformity of legislation produced a uniformity of government. It was therefore but a step for Congress, instead of passing enactments for the Territories separately, to enact laws which should affect the Territories as a whole, and this is the characteristic feature of the later legislation of Congress. Congress, however, did not proceed to this form of legislation until a most important question had been settled,—the question as to the extent of authority which it could exercise over the Territories. The question arose in the contention over the prohibition of slavery in the Territories.[2] The abolition of slavery

---

1. *Cf.* p. 15.

2. Johnston : Lalor's Political Encyclopædia, Article, Slavery. The essence of the struggle was simply were the Territories the property of " all the States " or of the "Nation."

throughout the United States furthered the claim of Congress to the right to enact such a prohibition. As a result of the war of 1861 the absolute control of the Territories by Congress was established.

Our Second Period thus falls into two divisions : The first extending from the organization of Wisconsin in 1836 until the establishment of the principle of absolute control in 1867 ; and the second extending from that date to the present, during which time the characteristic feature is the legislation for the Territories as a whole.

The Principle of Absolute Control of the Territories by Congress Established. 1836-1867.

It is the form of the Wisconsin Act that is important. The Territory that was organized included all of the present States of Wisconsin, Minnesota and Iowa, and a large part of North and South Dakota. It thus contained all that remained of the old " Northwest." The government that was established was based on the ordinance that had been enacted in 1787 to organize that " Northwest " as a Territory. But the Ordinance of 1787 was no longer fitted to serve as a Territorial organic act. In spite of the broadness and universality of its provisions, and in spite of the great services it had rendered and was still rendering, as an instrument of government it had become anti. quated. Some of its clauses had been embodied in the Federal constitution and no longer needed to be specified for a government that must be administered under that constitution, many of its principles had been changed, and it had been found necessary to treat all of the topics in greater detail.

The Orleans Act of 1804 was the first Territorial organic act in which Congress had dared to deviate from the lines of the Ordinance of 1787. It remained in force only one year, but the first step had been taken, and in the new act that was passed for Louisiana in 1805, as we have already seen, the difference in form was more important than the slight deviation from the Ordinance in the government that it established. This form of enactment had been further developed in the act for Missouri in 1812 and in the act for Arkansas of 1819. It was then upon the outlines of the Orleans Act of 1804, as modified by the acts for Missouri and Arkansas, that the Wisconsin Act of 1836 was modeled.

The act is divided into seventeen sections,[3] thirteen of which are devoted, respectively, to the governor; secretary; delegate to Congress; general assembly; its powers; restrictions on its members; exercise of the suffrage; election and appointment of local officials; organization of the judiciary; attorney and marshal; appointment and qualifications of the governor, secretary and judges—their salaries and expenses of the legislature; establishment of Territorial boundaries; and location of seat of government. Of the four remaining sections three were of only local importance and may in this connection be disregarded. The fourth, however, extended to the inhabitants all the rights, privileges and advantages, and subjected them to all the conditions, restrictions and prohibitions contained in the articles of compact of the Ordinance of 1787. The chief object of this was, of course, the prohibition of slavery.

As to the government established by this act, there are but four points to which attention should be called :[4]

1). Every free white male citizen of the United States, twenty-one years of age, and an inhabitant of the Territory at the time of its organization, was permitted to vote at the first election and was declared eligible to any office, but the qualifications of voters at all subsequent elections were left to the legislature to determine; provided, that

---

3. This division of the act into sections, made necessary by the greater detail as to the administration of the government, is of the greatest importance for the legislation that followed. This feature was so closely followed in the later organic acts that it would be possible to institute a comparison between the various Territorial governments by simple reference to the numbers of the sections of each act. *Cf.* Fisk: Stimmrecht und Einzelstaat in den Vereinigten Staaten von Nord Amerika. Leipzig 1896. p. 103. n. 2.

4. See Appendix B. 116).

the right of suffrage should be exercised only by citizens of the United States.

2). The governor's veto power was unqualified.

3). The members of council and of the house of representatives were to be elected for four years and two years respectively, and

4). The superior judges, appointed by the President were to hold office during good behavior.

Florida was the only Territory that remained from those of the First Period. Shortly after the organization of the Wisconsin Territory (April 20, 1836), Congress disapproved and annulled three acts specifically, and all other acts and parts of acts passed by the legislature of Florida during the year 1836 creating banks or corporations with banking powers, or conferring banking powers on any corporation or institution whatever.[5] Congress then further ordered, in the same act, that no act of the legislature of any Territory incorporating any bank, or any institution with banking powers or privileges, should have any force until approved and confirmed by Congress.

In 1838 all that part of the Territory of Wisconsin that was west of the Mississippi river was organized as the Territory of Iowa.[6] The act was an exact copy of the Wisconsin act, except that : the members of council were to be elected for two years, and members of the house for one ; and the judges of the superior court were to be appointed for four years.[7]

Ten years then elapsed before another Territory was established and during that time the enactments relate almost exclusively to the Territorial legislatures.[8] The legislature of Florida was reorganized on the plan of those of Iowa and Wisconsin ;[9] the terms of the members of the Florida and Wisconsin legislatures were made the same as in Iowa ;[10] the legislatures of Wisconsin

---

5. *Cf.* Appendix B. 31).   6. June 12, 1838.

7. See Appendix B. 121).   8. *Cf.* Appendix B. 122)—141).

9. Hitherto a legislature of one house. See Appendix B. 127).

10. Appendix B. 127) and 137).

and Iowa were given the same power as in Florida to overrule the governor's veto by a two-thirds vote;[11] and in 1842 the Territorial legislatures were forbidden to hold sessions until the appropriation for their expenses had been made by Congress,[12] and certain restrictions were passed upon the expenditure of these appropriations.

In the seventeen years from 1848 to 1864 thirteen new Territories were organized: Oregon, 1848; Minnesota, 1849; New Mexico and Utah, 1850; Washington, 1853; Nebraska and Kansas, 1854; Colorado, Nevada and Dakota, 1861; Arizona and Idaho, 1863; and Montana, 1864. All the governments established were closely modeled after Wisconsin except for such changes as were due to the permitting of slavery in certain of the Territories and in the following particulars: The judges of the superior court were to serve for four years instead of during good behavior; the governor was appointed for four years instead of three;[13] and the governor's veto power was sometimes absolute and sometimes limited[14] Further in Oregon, the upper house of the legislature was to consist of nine members to serve for three years, one-third of whom were to go out of office every year. The power of the legislature to incorporate banks or institutions with banking powers was denied, and the legislature was forbidden to borrow money in the name of the Territory or to pledge the faith of the people of the same for any loan

---

11. Appendix B. 130).

12. Some trouble over expenses of Wisconsin and Florida legislature seems to have arisen. See Appendix B. 136) and 134).

13. By Ordinance of 1787 governor appointed for three years and secretary for four. So until Oregon—when governor's term was made four years and the secretary's five. In Minnesota both appointed for four years, and so always since then, except in Kansas and Nebraska, where their terms were the same as in Oregon.

14. By organic acts veto power was unqualified in Oregon, New Mexico, Utah, Washington, Colorado, Nevada, Dakota and Arizona, in the others it could be overruled (always by two-thirds vote). The veto power was afterward limited: Colorado and Dakota in 1863, Washington in 1864, New Mexico in 1868 and Arizona in 1876.

whatever.[15] And these same modifications were enacted for Washington Territory[16] when it was cut off from Oregon in 1853.[17]

As Wisconsin, Iowa, Oregon and Minnesota were organized, the articles of compact of the Ordinance of 1787 were put in force.[18] When, however, the Territories of New Mexico and Utah were formed in 1850[19] it was enacted for each that, when admitted as a State, the Territory or any portion of it, should be received into the Union, with or without slavery, as their constitution should at the time prescribe. This necessitated further, in the organization of the judiciary, the provision that there should be writs of error and appeals to the Supreme Court of the United States in all cases involving the title to slaves, without regard to the amount in controversy, and upon any writ of habeas corpus involving the question of personal freedom. The judges of the supreme and district courts were also authorized to grant writs of habeas corpus in all cases in which the same were grantable by the judges of the United States in the District of Columbia. These same provisions were enacted for Nebraska and Kansas in 1854.[20] In establishing the

---

15. See further Appendix B. 143).   16. See further Appendix B, 158).

17. In 1866 Washington legislature made the same as in the other Territories. See Appendix B. 196).

18. See p. 40, *supra*.

19. See further Appendix B. 148) and 149).

20. In the Kansas-Nebraska act it was further provided, that nothing of this should be construed to affect the fugitive slave act of 1793, or the act of 1850 supplementary to it, both of which were declared to be in full force in these Territories. The section which declared the Constitution and laws of the United States to have the same force and effect in these Territories as elsewhere in the United States excepted "the eighth section of the act prepatory to the admission of Missouri into the Union, approved March sixth, eighteen hundred and twenty, which, being inconsistent with the principle of non-intervention by Congress with slavery in the States and Territories, as recognized by the legislation of eighteen hundred and fifty, commonly called the compromise measures," which was thereby decared inoperative and void ; "it being the true intent and

Territories of Colorado, Nevada and Dakota (1861), no reference was made to slavery.[21]

On June 19, 1862, it was enacted that there should be neither slavery nor involuntary servitude in any of the Territories of the United States, now existing or which may at any time hereafter be formed or acquired by the United States, otherwise than in the punishment of crimes whereof the party shall have been duly convicted. Accordingly as the Territories of Arizona, Idaho and Montana were organized in 1863-4 slavery was specifically prohibited.[22]

The statute which closes this first division of our second period was passed on January 24, 1867. It ordered that there should be no denial of the elective franchise in any of the Territories of the United States, now or hereafter to be organized, to any citizen thereof, on account of race, color, or previous condition of servitude.

Aside from the organization of the Territories that have been mentioned, the legislation of Congress relating to the Territories during all this time was of little importance. There was a general increase in the salaries paid to the Territorial officers by the United States,[23] and it was ordered that when an officer should absent himself from the Territory and his official duties for more than sixty days, his salary for that time should not be paid.[24]

---

meaning of this act not to legislate slavery into any Territory or State, nor to exclude it therefrom, but to leave the people thereof perfectly free to form and regulate their domestic institutions in their own way, subject only to the Constitution of the United States : Provided, That nothing herein contained shall be construed to revive or put in force any law or regulation which may have existed prior to the act of March sixth, eighteen hundred and twenty, either protecting, establishing, prohibiting, or abolishing slavery." See further Appendix B. 182).

21. See Appendix B. 176), 177) and 178).

22. See Appendix B. 184), 188) and 192).

23. See Appendix B. Organic Acts of Territories and 145), 163), 167), 171).

24. See Appendix B. 153), 156), and 157.)

Bigamy was forbidden in all the Territories,[25] and by the same act religious, etc., corporations were forbidden to hold more than $50,000 real estate.

Legislation for the Territories as a Whole.

The characteristic feature of the legislation from the time of the settlement of the slavery question down to the present day is, as we have said, the legislation for the Territories as a whole, *i. e.* instead of enacting laws for each Territory with regard to the special requirements of that district, Congress enacts but one law affecting all the Territories alike. Uniformity of government in the Territories was a prerequisite to such legislation, and this uniformity we have seen established since the organization of Wisconsin. The abolition of slavery destroyed the last great dividing line that had existed between the Territories.

The greatest uniformity had always existed in the judicial systems of the various Territories, owing to their common subordination to the Supreme Court of the United States. When, therefore, a uniform system of bankruptcy throughout the United States was established, and jurisdiction was to be given to the Territorial superior courts, it was but natural, with the similarity of their judiciaries, that Congress should include all the Territories in the one enactment. And so it was done.[26] The supreme courts of the Territories were given the same jurisdiction and powers as were vested in the United States district courts ; that is, they were made courts of bankruptcy with original jurisdiction. The declaration of Congress that it was not necessary in Territorial courts to exercise separately the common-law and chancery jurisdictions ;[27] the transferring of the jurisdiction in bankruptcy cases from the supreme courts to the district courts of the Territories ;[28] and the granting of writs of error or

---

25. See Appendix B. 181.)

26. March 2, 1867 (*cf.* Appendix B. 133).

27. April 7, 1874.   28. June 22, 1874.

appeals from the Territorial supreme courts to the supreme courts of the United States only when the amount in controversy was over $5,000,[29]—in each case by one enactment for all the Territories—are mainly proofs of the similarity of the Territorial judiciaries,[30] but they are at the same time indicative of the general Territorial legislation to which we wish to call attention.

This feature of legislation, however, is better exemplified in the enactments touching the legislatures. In most of the Territories members of the upper and lower houses were elected repectively for two years and one year. In some, the sessions had been made biennial, and there the terms had been lengthened to four and two years.[31] In 1868 it was enacted that in all the Territories the sessions should be biennial—or rather a proviso was attached to the Appropriation Act, that the amounts therein appropriated for the expenses of the legislative assemblies should only be expended for biennial sessions[32]—, and the following year it was added that the members of both houses should be elected for the term of two years.[33] A few years later it was ordered that the expense for printing for any session of the legislature of any Territory should not exceed $4,000.[34] In 1873[35] the sessions of all the Territorial legislatures were limited to forty days, the amount per day which the members were to receive, the mileage, the extra amount which the president of the council and the speaker of the house should receive, and also the salaries of the governors and secretaries were made by this one law the same for all Territories, and it was ordered that no law should be passed by a Territorial legislature by which officers would receive compensation other than that given by the laws of the United States. The next year it was required that the

---

29. March 3, 1885.
30. *Cf.* Appendix B. 27), 28), 48), 49)
31. See Appendix B. 196), 200), 204).
32. July 20, 1868.   33. March 3, 1869.   34. May 8, 1872.
✓ 35. See Appendix B. 247).

President should approve the reason for it, before an extraordinary session of any legislature could be called.[36] Finally in 1878 a clause was attached to the appropriation act, the main provisions of which remain in force to-day.[37] According to it the members of council were not to exceed twelve in number, nor the house twenty-four.[38] The members of each house were to receive $4 per day and mileage, the president of council and speaker of house $6. Each legislature was allowed one chief clerk, four subordinate clerks and a chaplain, for all of whom the salaries were fixed, and the expense of public printing was limited to $2,500.[39] In 1880 the limit of the sessions was extended to sixty days.[40]

The acts which have just been enumerated are all restrictions upon the Territorial legislatures, but only as regards their expenses or the length and frequency of their sessions. There were further limitations placed by Congress and in another direction, viz., Upon the power of incorporating and the passing of special acts, and these enactments are equally charactcristic of the feature of legislation to which we have called attention. The only previous legislation on this subject was the act in 1836,[41] by which no act of any Territorial legislature incorporating any bank or any institution with banking powers or privileges should have force or effect until approved by Congress, and the specification in the organic acts of Oregon and Washington,[42] that no power was therein contained to incorporate banks or institutions with banking powers. Now, however, in 1867 the legislative assemblies of all the Territories were forbidden to grant private charters or especial privileges, though they might by general acts permit persons to associate themselves together for mining, manufacturing or other industrial pursuits.[43]

---

36. June 22, 1874.   37. June 19, 1878.
38. *Cf.* Appendix B. 286) and 309).
39. See Appendix B. 270) and *cf.* 280).
40. December 23, 1880.   41. See p. 41 *supra*.
42. See pp. 42 and 43.   43. March 2, 1867.

This act of 1867 was the basis of all later legislation on the subject. For a time Congress seems to have been uncertain as to the extent to which the Territories should be permitted to incorporate even by general acts. In 1872, for example, four different railroad companies organized under the laws of Dakota, Utah, Colorado and New Mexico were granted right of way through the lands of the United States, but in each act it was specified that nothing therein should be construed or recognizing or denying the right of the said Territory to incorporate railroad companies. [44] When the question was finally decided in favor of the Territories, it was enacted in the form, that the Act of 1867 should be construed as authorizing the incorporation by general acts for railroads and wagon roads, and for educational, charitable and scientific associations. [45] It was later declared that this provision did not prohibit the Territorial legislatures from creating municipal corporations and conferring on them the necessary administrative powers, either by general or special acts. [46] And in 1885 this provision was amended so as to include banks and canals. [47]

The final act on the competence of Territorial legislatures in this respect was passed July 30, 1886. In it there were twenty-four subjects enumerated such as divorce, practice in courts of justice, taxes, rate of interest, and municipal corporations, upon which the Territorial legislatures were forbidden to pass local or special laws, and in all other cases where a general law could be made applicable. No Territory or subdivision of any Territory was allowed to subscribe to the capital stock of any corporation, or loan its credit for the benefit of any such association. The Territories were forbidden to incur debt except in certain special cases, and for penal, charitable or educational institutions, provided the total indebtedness did not thereby exceed 1% of the assessed value of taxable property. The limit of local indebted-

---

44. See Appendix B. 238), 239), 241) and 242).
45. June 10, 1872.
46. June 8, 1878.   47. March 3, 1885.

ness was placed at 4%. And the previous statutes relating to incorporation were amended to include insurance, banks of discount and deposit (but not of issue), loan, trust and guarantee associations.

Aside from this general legislation which has been given, the enactments of Congress relating to the individual Territories are of little importance. Additional superior judges were created in several of the Territories,[48] but this involved no changes other than the redistricting of the Territory in question. A tendency to increase the jurisdiction of the probate courts and justices of the peace is also noticeable.[49] The Territory of Wyoming was organized in 1868[50] and the Territory of Oklahoma in 1890[51] but as was to be inferred from the legislation which we have considered the organic acts of these Territories contain nothing new.[52] Only as regards Utah were the special enactments of Congress of any importance. There in order to stamp out polygamy Congress found it necessary to exercise to the full its absolute power. The courts were reorganized, and writs of error from the United States Supreme Court were allowed in cases of polygamy. The election of probate judges was taken out of the hands of the legislature, and their appointment given to the President. Law after law of the Territorial legislature was annulled. All the registration and election offices were declared vacant, the election districts and apportionment were abolished, and commissioners were appointed to redistrict and reapportion the Territory. A test oath was required before voting or holding office, and a board of five persons was appointed by the President to take charge of the registration of voters and the conduct of elections. But these acts are of general significance only as showing what Congress can do, and

---

48. See Appendix B. 273), 287), 296), 299), 302) and 306).

49. See Appendix B. 199), 218), 228), 259), 283), 289), *cf.* 309).

50. See Appendix B. 206).   51. See Appendix B. 309).

52. The District of Columbia was organized as a Territory in 1871. See Appendix C.

has done, when the occasion arises to exercise its final power of control. [53]

IV.

There are at present three organized Territories in the United States, New Mexico, Arizona and Oklahoma, established respectively 1850, 1863 and 1890, the governments of which, as we have seen, are practically identical. In each of these three Territories the executive, legislative and judicial departments are distinct from one another. The executive function is exercised by a governor and secretary, the legislative by a legislature of two houses, and the judicial by a supreme court and certain inferior courts. The governor, secretary and superior judges are appointed by the President. And finally each Territory sends a delegate to Congress, who is given a seat in the House of Representatives, with the right of speaking, but not of voting. Thus in its general features the Territorial government of to-day is the same as that established by the Ordinance of 1787, but within this framework the very greatest changes have taken place. [1]

First of all, the entire organization of the Territorial government has been more thoroughly perfected. In the executive department, some of the governor's powers have been taken away, upon others serious restrictions have been placed, and all of his rights and duties, as well as those of the secretary are clearly defined. In the legislative department, the composition of the general assembly, the length and frequency of its sessions, and the amount of expenses which it may incur have all been definitely established, and here also limitations have been placed, although the sphere of legislation which still remains to

---

53. See Appendix B. 259), 279) and 301).

1. *Cf.* Bryce: American Commonwealth. I. chap. XXXVIII. Many of the tendencies there pointed out apply to the Organic Acts of the Territories, which may be regarded as Territorial Constitutions.

the general assembly is very wide. In the judiciary, which originally consisted of three judges, two of whom were necessary to form a court with common-law jurisdiction, we find now a complete system of superior and inferior courts with appeals from the lower to the higher, and with appeal from the Territorial supreme court to the Supreme Court of the United States.

Secondly, the whole system of government has become more democratic. Property qualifications have been abolished for all offices to which the President appoints. The suffrage at the first election is granted to all male citizens of the United States, twenty-one years of age, residing in the Territory at the time of its organization, and the electoral franchise for all subsequent elections as well as the qualifications for office are left to the Territorial legislature to determine. Both houses of the legislature and the delegate to Congress have been made elective by the people, while justices of the peace, militia officers and all local officers are left to the legislature, to provide for their election or appointment. And the principle of " rotation in office," so thoroughly implanted in the popular mind as necessary to a democratic government, has brought about a marked shortening of the terms of all Territorial officials.[2] In the case of those appointed by the President the spoils system has brought them all into conformity with his term, even the judges having been changed from life tenure to the four year limit.[3]

Thirdly, there is a great increase in the salaries paid to all officials. In 1789 the governor received $2,000, the secretary $750, and the judges $800 each, and the expenses of the legislature were left to the Territory.[4] Now the governor is paid $3,500 (Oklahoma $2,600), the secretary

2. Bryce : *loc. cit.* II. p. 133 *et seq.*
3. " Though created by Congress they do not fall within the provisions of the Constitution for a Federal judiciary." Bryce : I. p. 581.
4. The members of the legislature in the Territory south of the Ohio received in 1794, $2.50 per day and $2.50 mileage. Ramsey : Annals of Tennessee, p. 623 *et seq.*

$2,500 (Oklahoma $1,800), the judges $3,000 each, and the members of the legislature receive $4 per day[5] and $4 for every twenty miles traveling expenses, the president of the council and speaker of the house receive an extra amount, salaries are paid to five clerks and a chaplain for each house, a "sufficient sum" is granted for the costs of printing, etc., and $1,000 is put into the hands of the governor for "contingent expenses."[6]

And finally, the absolute and unlimited authority of Congress over the Territories has become established.[7] It may govern mediately or immediately, either by the creation of a Territorial government with power to legislate for the Territory, subject to such restraints and limitations as Congress may impose upon it, or by the passage of laws directly operating upon the Territory, without the intervention of a subordinate government.[8] The contrary contention, that the inhabitants of a Territory have the entire control of their own local concerns, and may form their government independently of the national legislature has been distinctly repudiated by the Supreme Court.[9]

With this authority, as we have seen, Congress has organized twenty-eight Territories with greater or less powers of self-government, and has enacted laws for the further regulation of these governments in unbroken continuity from 1789 down to the present day. The object of this organization of Territories and of this further legislation has been a double one: to provide some form of civil authority, absolutely necessary to organize and preserve civilized society, and to prepare the

---

5. January 23, 1873. Members were allowed $6 per day, etc. See Appendix B. 247).

6. It is comforting to know that there was a time when Congress looked upon the cost of a Territory as an item to be considered. In 1808 the inhabitants of Indiana petitioned for the division of the Territory. One of the three reasons given for not granting the petition was "the unpromising aspect of our fiscal concerns." Annals of Congress, April 11, 1808.

7. Murphy vs. Ramsey. 114 U. S. 15. Story: loc. cit. II. p. 200.

district to become a State and a member of the Union. It is the latter that is the unique feature of the American colonial system.[10] That the Territories are to be regarded as inchoate States, as future members of the Union, has been and is the fundemental basis of our Territorial system. We have seen how this idea was first broached by a delegate from Maryland in Congress in 1777, how it was insisted upon by that State in her later declarations, how it was adopted by Congress, in its resolution of 1780, how it was embodied by some of the States in the acts ceding their western lands, and how it was approved by all of the States in accepting those cessions. In attempting to carry out this idea it was felt that the Congress under the Confederation was exerting strictly speaking an extra-constitutional power, and one of the great inducements to the adoption of the Constitution of 178 / 1789 was to give the 'general government adequate power to dispose of the western territory and admit new States into the Union. Finally in the treaty with France by which we acquired Louisiana, in the treaty with Spain ceding to us the Floridas, in the treaty with Mexico concluded at Guadalupe Hidalgo and in that by which we obtained "the Gadsden Purchase," there were provisions that the Territories ceded should be incorporated into the Union.[11]

Of the thirty-two States that have been admitted into the Union since 1789, twenty-six were permitted to organize themselves as States only after they had passed through the Territorial stage.[12] In the first ordinance for the gov-

8 American Insurance Company vs. Canter. I. Peters, 511. Edwards vs. Panama. I. Oregon, 418.

9. Pomeroy: Constitutional Law, p. 403.

10. Johnston ; loc. cit. Art. Territories.

11. See Appendix B. 18), 72), 142) and 161). In the treaty by which we acquired Alaska, on the other hand, this provision was omitted because there was no immediate prospect of the country becoming civilized enough to warrant the formation of Territories for ultimate incorporation as States in the Union.

12. See Appendix A.

ernment of the Territories, Jefferson's of 1784, the settlers were at first authorized only " to adopt the constitution and laws of any one of the original States," and not until a legislature had been formed were they permitted to change these laws. Similarly in the Ordinance of 1787 until a legislature was organized the governor and judges were only allowed " to adopt such laws of the original States as were best suited to the circumstances of the district." Experience is the best teacher The inhabitants of a Territory were not to be permitted to enact laws for themselves until they had become familiar with the way of doing things in the original States, and when they were allowed a measure of self-government it had to be exercised under a framework of government modeled on that which our fathers had found to be good. That Congress since 1789 has carried on the work in the spirit and with the purposes of the Ordinance of 1787, and has simply expanded this framework of Territorial government on the same lines that the whole country has developed, it has been the object of this paper to show. When a Territory was intrusted with the organization of its own government, reliance was placed on the conservatism of the people, and of the twenty-six Territories that have organized themselves as States there is not a single instance of one having substantially altered the form of government to which they were accustomed.[13]

This feature of policy thus stands embodied in the highest law of the land, it has been approved in the decisions of the Supreme Court, and it has been sanctioned by the experience of over a hundred years as one of the wisest provisions of our government.

---

13. California affords an example of a State which, entering the Union without having had the experience of a Territory, has encountered great difficulties in the regulation and administration of its government.

APPENDIX A.

Territory of	Was organized	Was admitted as State of	on
Northwest	July 13, 1787		
	August 7, 1789	Ohio	November 29, 1802
South	May 26, 1790	Tennessee	June 1, 1796·
Mississippi	April 7, 1798	Mississippi	December 10, 1817
Indiana	May 7, 1800	Indiana	December 11, 1816
Orleans	March 26, 1804	Louisiana	April 30, 1812
Louisiana	March 26, 1804	Became Territory of Missouri in 1812	
Michigan	January 11, 1805	Michigan	January 26, 1837
Illinois	February 3, 1809	Illinois	December 3, 1818
Missouri	June 4, 1812	Missouri	August 10, 1821
Alabama	March 3, 1817	Alabama	December 14, 1819
Arkansas	March 2, 1819	Arkansas	June 15, 1836
Florida	March 30, 1822	Florida	March 3, 1845
Wisconsin	April 20, 1836	Wisconsin	May 29, 1848
Iowa	June 12, 1838	Iowa	December 28, 1846
Oregon	August 14, 1848	Oregon	February 14, 1859
Minnesota	March 3, 1849	Minnesota	May 11, 1858
New Mexico	September 7, 1850		
✓Utah	September 9, 1850	Utah	January 4, 1896 ⌐
Washington	March 2, 1853	Washington	November 11, 1889
Nebraska	May 30, 1854	Nebraska	March 1, 1867
Kansas	May 30, 1854	Kansas	January 29, 1861
Colorado	February 28, 1861	Colorado	August 1, 1876
Nevada	March 2, 1861	Nevada	October 31, 1864
Dakota	March 2, 1861	{ North Dakota { South Dakota	} November 2, 1889
Arizona	February 24, 1863		
Idaho	March 3, 1863	Idaho	July 3, 1890
Montana	May 26, 1864	Montana	November 8, 1889
Wyoming	July 25, 1868	Wyoming	July 11, 1890
Oklahoma	May 2, 1890		

Admission of Territories into the Union.

The organization of a Territory as a State and its admission into the Union is dependent upon the will of Congress alone By the articles of compact of the Ordinance of 1787 the Territories of the Northwest were granted the right to organize themselves as States and to be admitted into the Union as soon as their population should amount to 60,000. Upon this basis the Territories of the Northwest and those in the South, over which the Ordinance of 1787 was extended, were allowed to organize themselves as States and were received into the Union. With the enormous increase of population throughout the United States, this number was found to be too small, and a population equal to an average Congressional district was usually required. Congress has, however, absolute discretion in the matter and often makes very arbitrary use of its power. Nevada, for example, was admitted as a State in 1864 when its population was only about 20,000. In 1872 it was enacted that no State should be admitted to the Union without having the necessary population to entitle it to one representative, which according to the census of 1890 would require a population of about 174,000.

APPENDIX B.

ACTS OF CONGRESS RELATING TO THE GOVERNMENT OF THE ORGANIZED TERRITORIES OF THE UNITED STATES.

1) 1789, August 7.   Ordinance of 1787 re-enacted. Instead of Congress, President, with Senate. to appoint officers, etc.; in absence of governor, secretary to act with power. See p. 14. For provisions of Ordinance, see pp. 8 *et seq.*

2) ·1789, Sept. 11.   In Northwest Territory, Governor's salary and for superintendent of Indian affairs, $2,000. Judges, $800 each. Secretary, $750.

3) 1790, April 2.   Cession of North Carolina accepted, see p. 17.

4) 1790, May 26.   Government established in same, see p. 17. Salaries as in Northwest Territory. Governor to be superintendent of Indian affairs.

5) 1792, May 8.   Laws of Northwest Territory to be published. Governor and judges authorized to repeal their own laws, see p. 19, N. 20. One superior judge may hold court. Limitation act passed by governor and judges of Northwest Territory on Dec. 28, 1788, disapproved.

6) 1794, Dec. 3.   Delegate from South Territory admitted to seat in House, see p. 17

7) 1798, April 7.   To settle limits with the State of Georgia and establish a government in the Mississippi Territory, see p. 20. Salaries as in Northwest. Governor superintendent of Indian affairs.

8) 1800, Jan. 2.   Delegate from Northwest Territory, see p. 18.

9) 1800, May 7.   Territory· of Indiana organized, see pp. 19 and 20. Salaries as in Northwest, and governor superintendent of Indian affairs.

      Until 5,000 free male inhabitants number of representatives not to be less than seven nor more than nine, to be apportioned by governor to counties according to number of free males of age in each.

      Until otherwise ordered by legislatures, Chillicothe to be seat of government of Northwest, and Vincennes of Indiana.

10) 1800, May 10.   See p. 20. Mississippi allowed to organize a legislature. Until 5,000 inhabitants not to be more than nine representatives. Apportion-

ment made by counties. Date of election fixed.
Assembly to be held at Natchez on ———.
After 5,000 inhabitants, number and apportionment to be according to Ordinance. Governor to have power to convene on extraordinary
occasions. During sessions neither house to
adjourn, without consent of other, for more than
three days, nor to any other place. See also
p. 25.

11) 1800, Dec. 15. Franking privilege and compensation of
member of House granted to Harrison, and to
every other delegate from Northwest Territory.

12) 1801, Feb. 13. New Federal judiciary system established.
United States divided into six circuits. Ohio
and Indiana Territories to constitute one of the
four districts of the sixth circuit. See p. 22 N. 30.
Repealed March 8, 1802.

13) 1801, March 2. Suits and processes in Northwest and Indiana
Territories revived and continued as if North-
west Territory had been undivided.

14) 1802, Feb. 18. Privileges and compensation of Territorial
delegates to Congress. See pp 17 and 18.

15) 1802, April 29. Proceedings depending in circuit court
(established by act of February 13, 1801,
abolished by act of March 8, 1802,) to be continued in superior courts of Territories.

16) 1802, April 30. People of eastern division of Territory northwest of the Ohio authorized to form a constitu-
tion and State government.

17) 1803, April 30. Treaty with France ceding Louisiana signed.

18) 1803, Oct. 31 Treaty ratified. Art. 3. "The inhabitants
of the ceded territory shall be incorporated in
the Union of the United States, and admitted
as soon as possible, according to the principles
of the Federal Constitution, to the enjoyment
of all the rights, advantages, and immunities
of citizens of the United States ; and, in the
meantime, they shall be maintained and protected in the free enjoyment of their liberty,
property, and the religion which they profess."

19) 1803, Oct. 31. President to take possession of ceded Territory, see p. 20.

20) 1804, March 26. Establishing Territory of Orleans and District of Louisiana, see pp. 21-24. Further
provisions :

Orleans :—Legislature to establish inferior
courts. Salaries : governor $5,000 ; secretary
and judges $2,000, district Judge $2,000.
Attorney to receive $600 and fees, marshal $200.
All free white male house-keepers, resident
one year, qualified to serve as grand or petit
jurors. Unlawful to import slaves into Territory from without the limits of the United States.

District of Louisiana :— Governor to divide
into convenient districts Inhabitants of each,
between ages of 18 and 45, to be formed into a
militia. Commanding officer to be appointed
by President, others by the governor.

Twenty-one Federal acts named to be in
force in both.

21) 1804, March 27.   Act, regulating manner of authenticating
acts, records and judicial proceedings so as to
take effect in every other State, extended to the
Territories

22) 1804, March 27.   An additional judge for Mississippi Territory
with powers and salary of superior judges, but
not himself one of the superior court. Provisions relating to writs of error and appeals.

23) 1804, March 27.   Tract of country to the north added to the
Territory of Mississippi.

24) 1805, Jan. 11.   Michigan Territory established, see p. 25
Salaries as in Indiana. Detroit to be the seat
of government until changed by Congress.

25) 1805, March 2.   Orleans government to be as in Mississippi,
see p. 24. When Territory shall have 60,000
inhabitants to have right to form constitution
and State government. Until admitted as State,
Congress reserves right to change boundaries
of Territory at pleasure.

26) 1805, March 3.   District of Louisiana made the Territory of
Louisiana, see p. 24. Superior judges to be
appointed for four years.

27) 1805, March 3.   Jurisdiction of Territorial superior courts in
cases where United States a party, see p. 25.

28) 1806, April 18.   Compensation of jurors, marshals, etc.,
see p. 25.

29) 1807, March 3.   Salary of superior judges in Mississippi,
Indiana, Michigan and Louisiana $1,200.

30) 1807, March 3. $300 each to officers of Indiana for services in
District of Louisiana by act of March 27, 1804.

31) 1807, March 3.   Act of Governor and judges of Michigan "concerning Bank of Detroit" disapproved.

32) 1807, Dec. 5.   Salary of secretary in Mississippi, Indiana, Louisiana and Michigan to be $1,000.

33) 1808, Jan. 9.   Suffrage extended in Mississippi, see p. 25 and 26. General assembly authorized to apportion representatives to the several counties according to number of free white males in each. Until 6,000 free white males, whole number of representatives not to be less than 10 nor more than 12. After 6,000 inhabitants, number to be regulated by Ordinance.

34) 1808, Feb. 26.   Suffrage extended in Indiana, see p. 26.

35) 1809, Feb. 3.   Territory of Illinois cut off from Indiana. Government to be as in Indiana. Kaskaskia to be seat of government until changed by legislature.

36) 1809, Feb. 27.   Extension of suffrage and of offices elective in Indiana, see p. 26. And general assembly to apportion representatives, not more than 12 nor less than 9, until 6,000 inhabitants, when it shall be according to the Ordinance.

37) 1809, Dec. 15.   Governor to make temporary apportionment in Indiana. In case of vacancy in elective office governor to issue writ for new election.

38) 1810, March 2.   Suffrage extended to citizens of Madison county in Mississippi. Additional superior judge and court for said county. Appeals from courts in Washington and Madison counties to superior court in Adams county, which must consist of two judges when considering appeals. Legislature authorized to establish a superior court in each county within former district of Washington, with appeals to superior court of Adams county.

39) 1811, Jan. 15.   Act authorizing the President in certain events to take possession of the Floridas and to establish temporary government.

(On March 3, 1811, it was ordered that this act should not be printed until the end of the next session of Congress).

40) 1811, Feb. 20.   Enabling people of Orleans to form constitution and State government.

41) 1811, March 3.   Right of suffrage in Indiana further extended, see p. 26. Persons holding appointments

under governor of Indiana, except justices of peace and military officers, not eligible to legislature.

42)	1812, May 14.	Boundaries of Mississippi extended.
43)	1812, May 20.	Boundaries of Ohio, Indiana and Michigan to be ascertained.
44)	1812, May 20.	Legislature to be organized in Illinois. Suffrage extended, see p. 26. Representatives to be not more than 12 nor less than 7, and to be apportioned as in 36).
45)	1812, June 4.	Louisiana Territory changed into the Territory of Missouri see pp. 26, 27 and 28. Governor superintendent of Indian affairs, and had power to grant pardons and reprieves. To be 9 members of council, residents of one year, owning 200 acres, holding no office of profit, except justice of the peace, and must be 25 years of age. Number of representatives to be as in Ordinance, must be freeholders in county in which elected, residents of one year, and holding no office of profit under Territory. Each house to choose a speaker and its other officers, determine the rules of its proceedings, and sit on its own adjournments from day to day. Neither house, without consent of the other, to adjourn for more than two days, nor to any other place. Members free from arrest during sessions, and for speech in either house not to to be questioned in any other place. St. Louis the seat of government. All free white male residents of one year, unless disqualified by legal proceeding, qualified to serve as grand and petit jurors. Delegate elective. Salaries as before.
46)	1812, June 10.	Nothing in act of February 3d, 1809, dividing Indiana, to prevent issuing of executions on judgments and decrees rendered in that Territory.
47)	1812, June 17.	Resolution requesting Georgia to give assent to the formation of two States out of the Mississippi Territory.
48)	1812, Dec. 18.	Restrictions on district and Territorial judges, see p. 29. No judge appointed under the United States shall act as council or attorney or practice law.

49) 1813, Feb. 27.   An attorney for the United States and a marshal to be appointed in each Territory. Attorney to receive fees and $250. Marshal to receive same compensation as marshal of district of Kentucky.

50) 1814, Jan. 27.   Additional judge and court for the district of Arkansas in Territory of Missouri. Term 4 years. Same salary as superior judges. Jurisdiction of superior court and of court of common pleas. Appeals to superior court. Rules and conditions of the same. Two terms annually. Time and place fixed, but may be changed by general assembly.

51) 1814, March 4.   Indiana house of representatives to lay off Territory into five districts for election of members of council.

52) 1814, Oct. 25.   In Mississippi suffrage extended as in Missouri, see p. 26. To be four additional members of council.

53) 1814, Nov. 21.   If he think it necessary and expedient, the Secretary of State authorized to publish laws of United States in two newspapers in every Territory.

54) 1815, Feb. 24.   In Indiana the presence of two judges required for a court. Times and places of sessions fixed. No person acting under Territory to be associated with judges.

55) 1815, March 3.   Judiciary system in Illinois revised, see p. 29. No one to be associated with judges, as in 54).

56) 1816, April 19.   Indiana authorized to form constitution and State government.

57) 1816, April 20.   Duties of judges in Illinois further defined. 55) to remain in force only until end of next session of legislature, see p. 29. Chancery powers given to general court of Indiana.

58) 1816, April 29.   In Missouri, the Members of council to be elected. Sessions of general assembly biennial. General assembly authorized to require superior judges to hold circuit courts, with jurisdiction in all cases over $100, similar to those established in Illinois by 55), see p. 29.

59) 1817, March 1.   The western part of Mississippi authorized to form constitution and State government.

60) 1817, March 3.   Territorial delegates to be elected every second year, see p. 28. In Missouri, date of next election of delegate fixed. General

assembly authorized to provide by law for annual or biennial sessions as interests of Territory require. Sessions to be on first Monday in December unless different day be appointed by law (of Territory).

61) 1817, March 3. Eastern part of Mississippi Territory organized as Territory of Alabama. Government as in Mississippi, see p. 29. General assembly to elect delegate to Congress. St. Stephens to be seat of government, until otherwise ordered by legislature.

62) 1818, April 9. Purchasers of one quarter section of public land in Alabama to be eligible to hold any office.

63) 1818, April 18. Illinois authorized to form constitution and State government. Portion of Territory to be added to Michigan, when State formed.

64) 1818, April 20. Judiciary in Alabama, see pp. 29 and 30. Legislature to regulate times and places of superior courts in each county. All officers to take oath before entering on duties.

65) 1819, Feb. 16. Delegate in Michigan to be elected by free white males of age, residents of one year, who have paid county or Territorial tax.

66) 1819, March 2. Alabama authorized to form constitution and State government.

67) 1819, March 2. Territory of Arkansas cut off from Missouri and organized, see p. 29. Government as in Missouri, but legislative power vested in governor and judges Legislature to be organized on wish of majority of freeholders. Until 5,000 inhabitants, not to be more than 9 representatives. Salaries as in Missouri. Delegate to be elected when legislature formed. Arkansaw to be seat of government until otherwise ordered by legislative department.

68) 1819, March 3. President authorized to take possession of the Floridas, and establish temporary government. See 73), and p. 30.

69) 1820, March 6. Missouri authorized to form constitution and State government. In Territory ceded by France, slavery prohibited north of thirty-six degrees and thirty minutes north latitude. Fugitive slaves may be reclaimed.

70) 1820, April 21. Act 45) for Missouri, as modified by 58), to be in force in Arkansas, as far as may be applicable.

71) 1820, April 24.   Laws of Michigan to be printed and distributed.

72) 1821. Feb. 22.   Ratification of the treaty with Spain ceding the Floridas, which had been concluded February 22, 1819.

" Art. V. The inhabitants of the ceded territories shall be secured .in the free exercise of their religion, without any restriction * * *

" Art. VI. The inhabitants of the territories ceded by this treaty, shall be incorporated in the Union of the United States as soon as may be consistent with the principles of the Federal Constitution, and admitted to the enjoyment of all the privileges, rights, and immunities of the citizens of the United States."

73) 1821, March 3.   Act 68) re enacted, see 68), and p. 30.

74) 1822, March 30.   Territorial government organized in Florida, see pp. 30 and 20. Salaries : Governor, $2,500; secretary and judges, $1,500 each; members of council, $3 per day for attendance, and $3 mileage. Members of council free from arrest during sessions. Two attorneys and two marshals to be appointed. 24 acts of United States specified to be in force. Sessions of council to be held in Pensacola.

75) 1822, May 7.   Act made by general Jackson as governor, " providing for the naturalization of inhabitants of ceded territory," and an ordinance of city council of St. Augustine, laying certain taxes, and all others enforcing and confirming these, repealed by Congress.

76) 1823 Jan. 30.   Additional judge for Michigan. Within certain counties to possess jurisdiction of county courts and of Territorial supreme court. Appeals from county courts to this court, and from this court to Territorial supreme court. No cognizance of cases of admirality or maritime jurisdiction, nor cases where the United States are plaintiffs. Particulars regarding writs of error. Judge to reside in one of counties, and receive same salary as judges of supreme court.

77) 1823, March 3.   Act 74) for Florida revised and amended, see p. 31. Appointments of officers by governor to be made only with consent of council. Governor forbidden to leave Territory without first getting permission from President. Council to

meet at St. Augustine, or such place as governor and council may appoint. Proceedings of last session of Florida council confirmed, except the revenue laws imposing taxes on inhabitants or property, and law authorizing governor to borrow $5,000 on credit of Territory, all of which are declared null and void. Act, repealing all previous laws and ordinances in force, declared to have effect on day of passage by council, and not of its approval by governor. Under no circumstances were soldiers of the United States to be qualified to vote.

78) 1823, March 3. Changing government of Michigan, see p. 32. $2 mileage and $2 per day attendance. Legislature authorized to submit question to people and if majority of votes favored it, general assembly to be organized according to the Ordinance, except members of council to be elective and serve for four years. When legislature organized, until 5,000 free white males of age, whole number of representatives not to be less than 7 nor more than 9. To be apportioned in first case by governor to counties. After organization of assembly, to be apportioned by it. Until 6,000 inhabitants, number of representatives not to be more than 12 nor less than 7. After 6,000 inhabitants number to be regulated by the Ordinance.

79) 1824, April 9. Acts of James Miller, as governor of Arkansas from March 3, 1822, to January 3, 1823, confirmed.*

80) 1824, April 22. Assent of Congress given to act of Florida council, "for levying a poll tax."

81) 1824, May 26. Florida judicial system revised, see p. 33. To be three attorneys and marshals. Date of session of legistative council changed. Governor to be allowed to leave Territory without permission of President.

82) 1824, May 26. Western boundary of Arkansas fixed.

---

*Miller's term as governor expired and President forgot to reappoint him until 8 months later, hence the necessity of this act. In organic acts of Wisconsin 1836, and Iowa there is nothing but in organic act of Minnesota 1848, and in all acts since then, it reads for—years, "and until successor be appointed and qualified."

83) 1824, May 26.   District court in Missouri given jurisdiction in certain land cases. The same extended to superior court of Arkansas. For these services judges granted $800 yearly in addition to regular pay.

84) 1825, Feb. 5.   Act 78) for Michigan amended, see pp. 33 and 34. Council increased to 13. $3 for attendance and $3 mileage. Two judges necessary to hold court. Governor and council to divide Territory into townships and incorporate the same, etc.

85) 1825, March 3.   Concerning wrecks on the coast of Florida May be condemned in any court of the United States Territories having competent jurisdiction.

86) 1826, Feb. 1.   Act of Florida council "concerning wreckers and wrecked property" annulled by Congress.

87) 1826, May 4.   Boundary between Florida and Georgia to be marked.

88) 1826, May 15.   Amending the several acts for Florida. See p. 33. Governor to divide Territory into 13 districts, designate places for holding elections, appoint judges of election. Date of first election fixed. Governor and council to regulate it thereafter. Five acts passed by governor and council in December, 1825, disapproved.

89) 1827, Jan. 29.   Michigan legislative council made elective. See p. 34. Governor and council to apportion representatives. Governor and council authorized to provide for holding of one or more courts, by one or more judges of superior court, in each of the counties east of Lake Michigan; and to prescribe the jurisdiction and the powers and duties of the judges.

90) 1827, March 3.   Governor and council of Florida authorized to provide for holding superior courts at such other places as may be necessary for more convenient administration of justice.

91) 1828, April 17.   Additional judge for Arkansas. Term four years. When commissioned, legislature to organize the counties into four judicial districts, assign a judge to each, and require each to hold circuit or district courts in each county. To be two terms annually of superior court at seat of government. In all cases, except where United

States a party, legislature authorized to fix 'the jurisdiction of district and superior courts. Appeals from district courts to superior court, and from superior court to United States Supreme Court, where amount over $1,000. Appellate cases before the superior court to be tried by the judges, or any two of them, other than the judge who made the decision in the district court.

92) 1828, April 28. Date of session of Florida council changed. Proviso in act 77), that no act of council imposing tax should be in force unless approved by Congress (see p. 31), repealed. At next session governor and council ordered to district Territory for council members, and to alter these districts as population changed. Judges authorized to order extra terms, or to adjourn. One judge permitted to hold court for another when compelled to be absent.

93) 1828, May 19. President in conjunction with constituted authorities of State of Louisiana to run and mark boundary of Territory of Arkansas and State of Louisiana.

94) 1828, May 23. Jurisdiction of 83) given to Florida courts.

95) 1828. May 23. Another judicial district in Florida. Same jurisdiction as other superior courts of Florida. Subject to same laws. Attorney and marshal. Sessions fixed. Salary $2,000. Directions regarding salvage in certain cases.

96) 1828, May 24. Members of Arkansas legislature to be paid. $3 attendance, and $3 for every 25 miles of actual distance from residence to place of session, to be certified to by governor. $720 for incidental expenses of legislature. See p. 34.

97) 1829, Jan. 21. Citizens of Arkansas and Florida authorized to elect their officers, civil and military, except those appointed by the President, and justices of the peace, auditor and treasurer of Territory who were to be elected by joint vote of both houses of legislature. Terms, powers, duties, fees, and emoluments to be fixed by legislature. See p. 34. In Florida, members of councils increased to 16. Apportioned to the several counties, but governor and council authorized to re-apportion. Act of governor and council

fixing seat of justice of Jackson county annulled, and people of that county authorized to select their county seat, as permitted to other counties under laws of Territory.

98) 1830, April 2. To change, in Michigan, time and place of court for county of Crawford, held by the additional judge of the United States. See 76)

99) 1830, April 15. Additional brigadier general for Arkansas to be appointed by President.

100) 1830, May 8. Further judicial powers given in jurisdiction granted by 83).

101) 1830. May 8. In Arkansas, governor authorized to fill vacancies, in elective offices until next election, in offices filled by legislature until next session of legislature.

102) 1830, May 14. In Florida, date of session of legislative council changed. 1st and 3d sections of act "to amend an act for apprehension of criminals, etc." passed by governor and council, annulled.

103) 1831, March 2. To mark boundary line between State of Alabama and Territory of Florida, and to mark Northern boundary of State of Illinois.

104) 1832, March 22. To be two additional members of council in Florida.

105) 1832, May 31. Suffrage in Arkansas extended. See p. 34.

106) 1832, July 14. Court of appeals, in Florida, to consist of judges of superior courts. Majority necessary to hear and decide causes, but any two sufficient to grant orders and writs. Writs of error and appeals from highest court of law and equity in the Territory to Supreme Court of United States as from the highest court of law and equity in a State, according to 25th section of act of Sept. 24, 1789.

107) 1833, March 2. Legislative council of Michigan, then in session, authorized to prolong its session thirty days beyond time allowed by law. $2,000 appropriated for extra expense.

108) 1833, March 2. Legislative council of Michigan authorized to re-district Territory, to secure more equal representation in council. If council adjourn before April 1, governor to district Territory by proclamation.

109) 1834, June 18. New apportionment of members of Florida council made. Council forbidden to employ more than three clerks, nor have Territorial

laws printed in more than three newspapers at public expense. Secretary of Territory to superintend printing and revision of laws. Amount to be appropriated by council not to exceed $7,000, including pay, mileage and inci· dentals. Part of an act relating to printing and binding of laws, and 21st section of an act of 1834 relating to judicial proceedings, disapproved and annulled.

110) 1834, June 28. Territory west of the Mississippi and north of the Missouri attached to Michigan.

111) 1834, June 30. Michigan council authorized to hold extra session, when governor thinks proper. $3,000 appropriated for it.

112) 1834, June 30. Superior judges in Michigan, Arkansas, and Florida to receive $300 additional salary yearly. Not allowed to such judges in Florida and Arkansas as receive extra compensation for land cases by 83) and 94). To take effect with them when extra pay for land cases no longer allowed.

113) 1834, June 30. Acts of Florida council, imposing greater tax on slaves or other property of non-residents than on those of residents repealed. County of Leon to elect two additional members of council.

114) 1835, March 3. Company organized under act of governor and council of Florida authorized to construct a railroad upon public lands.

115) 1836, Feb. 25. Special term of court of appeals for Florida ordered. When regular term not held, judges may appoint special term. Slight changes made in two judicial districts.

116) 1836, April 20. Territory of Wisconsin organized, see pp. 89 *et seq.*

Act does not affect rights of Indians, nor inhibit Federal government from dividing as it pleases. Governor's term three years, secretary's four. Council to number 13, house 26; to be apportioned to counties according to population, except Indians. Governor to order first election and apportionment, but thereafter legislature to do all this, and fix date of annual sessions, but no session to be more than 75 days. Justices of peace not to have jurisdiction over $50. Members of legislature must be residents of district. No one holding commission under United States, except militia officers, eligible to office.

Salaries: as governor and superintendent of Indian affairs, $2,500; judges, $1,800; secretary, $1,200. Members of assembly $3 attendance, $3 mileage. $350 for contingent expenses to be expended by governor, and a sufficient sum for legislative expenses.

117) 1836, July 1. Restriction of legislative powers to incorporate banks, and to disapprove certain acts of Florida legislature, see p. 41.

118) 1836, July 2. Act of Florida council "to change terms of superior court for middle-district," approved. Act to amend the act "incorporating Appalachiola," and act to "change county seat of Franklin," and so much of an act as directs a superior court for southern district at Indian Key, are annulled.

119) 1837, Jan. 31. Similar to 114).

120) 1837, March 3. Acts of Wisconsin legislature incorporating three banks, approved, but on condition that none of them should issue bank notes until one half of capital paid in ; capital not to be more than $200,000 except with consent of Congress ; none to owe more than twice the amount of paid in capital above deposits.

121) 1838, June 12. Territory of Iowa organized. Same as Wisconsin 116), except :—see p. 41, and judges were to receive salary of $1,500. Governor temporarly to define districts and assign judges, but legislature may change at any time.

122) 1838, June 12. Joint resolution disapproving act of Wisconsin legislature incorporating State bank.

123) 1838, June 18. Assent of Congress given to act of Wisconsin incorporating the Milwaukee and Rock River Canal Company. Until Territory becomes a State, Congress may prescribe and regulate tolls to be received by said company, after admission of State, legislature to have that power.

124) 1838, June 12. Boundary line between State of Michigan and Territory of Wisconsin to be marked.

125) 1838, June 18. Southern boundry of Iowa to be ascertained.

126) 1838, June 28. Act of Florida incorporating Florida Peninsula Railroad and Steamboat Company approved, provided no banking privilege conveyed, and same proviso regarding regulation of tolls as above—123).

127) 1838, July 7.   Florida legislature reorganized, see p. 41·
                       House same as present council with 3 more.
                       Senate of 11 from judicial districts. $4 during
                       sessions, and $4 mileage. Senate may be in-
                       creased to 15. Date of election fixed. No
                       session over 75 days. Council may re-apportion
                       members of both houses.

128) 1838, July 7.   New judicial district (5th) ordered for Florida.
                       Judge, marshal and district attorney to be ap-
                       . pointed, same powers, jurisdiction and salaries
                       as in other superior courts in Florida.

129) 1839, March 3.   Judges salaries in Iowa to be the same as in
                       Wisconsin.

130) 1839, March 3.   Legislatures of Wisconsin and Iowa author-
                       ized to overrule governors veto, see pp. 41 and
                       42. Governor must return bills within 3 days.
                       This act does not affect power of Congress
                       over laws of Territorial assembly.

131) 1839, March 3.   Eastern boundary of Iowa to be defined.

132) 1839, March 3,   Iowa legislature to provide for election or
                       appointment of sheriffs, judges of probate, jus-
                       tices of peace, and county surveyors. *Cf.* 139)
                       and p. 36—6). Term of present delegate to
                       expire at certain date, date of next election
                       fixed and thereafter delegate to serve for a Con-
                       gress as members of the House of Repre-
                       sentatives.

133) 1841, Aug. 19.   Uniform system of bankruptcy throughout
                       the United States established. Superior courts
                       of Territories given same jurisdiction, power
                       and authority as United States district courts.
                       Repealed March 3, 1843.

134) 1842, May 18.   Clause in appropriation act, that the legisla-
                       tive assembly of no Territory should, under any
                       pretex whatever, exceed amount appropriated
                       by Congress for its annual expenses.

135) 1842, Aug. 11.   Judges in Iowa to be assigned to districts as
                       heretofore, until otherwise ordered by Terri-
                       torial assembly.

136) 1842, Aug. 29.   Proper officers of Treasury Department
                       directed to settle accounts of legislative assem-
                       blies of Wisconsin and Florida, and not to allow
                       extra compensation to members, except to pre-
                       siding officers, nor to secretary of Territory, nor
                       clerk of either house, see p. 42, N. 12. All
                       accounts of money appropriated by Congress

for Territories to be settled at Treasury Department. No payment to be made or allowed unless Secretary of Treasury have estimated therefore and object be approved by Congress. Charges to be allowed for 5 clerks, to none of whom shall more than $3 per day be paid. Secretary of Territory to prepare acts for printing, furnishing copy to public printer within ten days after passage of each act.

137) 1843, March 3.   Wisconsin legislature to provide for election or appointment of officers as in 132), *cf*. 139). At expiration of present terms, members of both houses to be elected for same terms as in Iowa.

138) 1844, April 30.   Extra session of Iowa legislature authorized provided, government of United States bear no portion of expense.

139) 1844, June 15.   Territorial legislatures authorized to reapportion representation, and justices of peace and all general militia officers to be elected by people.

140) 1844, June 17.   Commissioner for Iowa to be appointed to meet with commissioner from Missouri to ascertain boundary line between Iowa and Missouri.

141) 1846, Aug. 6.   Territory of Wisconsin authorized to form constitution and State government.

142) 1848, Feb. 2.   TREATY OF GUADALUPE HIDALGO. Ratifications exchanged at Queretaro, May 30, 1848. Proclaimed July 4, 1848. By this treaty the United States acquired territory lying between the Rio Grande river north along the 106th meridian of longitude west from Greenwich to the 42d parallel north latitude, and along that parallel to the Pacific Ocean.

Article IX.

" The Mexicans who, in the territories aforesaid, shall not preserve the character of citizens of the Mexican Republic, conformably with what is stipulated in the preceding article, shall be incorporated into the Union of the United States, and be admitted at the proper time (to be judged of by the Congress of the United States) to the enjoyment of all the rights of citizens of the United States, according to the principles of the Constitution, and in the meantime shall be maintained and protected in the free enjoyment of their liberty and property, and secured in the free exercise of their religion without restriction.

143) 1848, Aug. 14.   Territory of Oregon organized. See pp. 42
and 43. Lower house of legislature of 18, might
be increased to 30, for 1 year. No session more
than 60 days, except first might be 100. Legislature to provide for appointment or election
of all township, district, and county officers not
otherwise provided for. Judges to serve for 4
years. Justices of peace not to have jurisdiction in land cases or where amount over $100.
Appeals from superior court to United States
Supreme Court only where over $2,000. Salar-
ies, governor $1,500, and $1,500 as superintendent of Indian affairs; judges, $2,000, secre-
tary, $1,500. Members of legislature $3 per day
attendance and $3 mileage. Chief clerk $5 and
3 other clerks $3 per day for each house. Speci-
fied that all taxes should be equal, no distinc-
tion in assessments between different kinds of
property. Every law should embrace but one
object and have that expressed in the title. No
one in army or navy ever to hold civil office, and
not to be allowed to vote until after six months
residence. Mileage of delegate to Congress
limited to $2,500. Existing laws now in force
in the Territory of Oregon under authority of
provisional government established by the
people thereof, to be in force until otherwise
ordered by the legislature.

144) 1849, March 3.   Territory of Minnesota organized, see pp. 42
and 43. 9 members of upper house, 18 of lower.
No session over 60 days. Justices of peace
given jurisdiction up to $100. Salary of secre-
tary, $1,800. Ordinance of 1787 extended over
Territory. Legislature not empowered to fix
permanent seat of government for the Territory,
but were to arrange by law for submitting that
question to a vote of the people.

145) 1850, June 5.   In Oregon, superintendent of Indian affairs
separated from governor. Governor's salary
$3,000.

146) 1850, July 18.   Governors of Oregon and Minnesota to report to Congress annually detailed statement
of expenditure of appropriations of Congress
for Territories, expended by governor and
assembly.

147) 1850, July 18. Minnesota and Oregon authorized to prolong next annual session of legislatures to 90 days.

148) 1850, Sept. 9. Territory of New Mexico organized, see pp. 42 and 43. Term of governor, secretary and judges 4 years. Council of 13, 2 years ; house of 26, 1 year. Apportionment according to population Indians excepted   40 days limit of sessions. No one holding commission under United States, except postmasters, eligible for office. Salaries: As governor, $1,500; and as superintendent of Indian affairs, $1,000; judges and secretary, $1,800 each; members of assembly, $3 per day attendance and $3 mileage. $1,000 for contingent expenses. Sufficient sum for legislative. Mileage of delegate limited as from Oregon.

No citizen of United States shall be deprived of his life, liberty, or property in Territory, except by judgment of his peers and law of the land.

149) 1850, Sept. 9. Territory of Utah organized, exactly same as for New Mexico, except last section omitted.

150) 1850, Sept. 18. Territorial superior courts given same power as United States circuit courts, in appointing commissioners, etc., relating to fugitive slaves.

151) 1850, Sept. 20. Clause in deficiency appropriation act. Mileage of delegate from Oregon to be computed according to the most usually traveled route within the limits of the United States.

152) 1851, Feb. 19. Legislatures of Minnesota and Oregon authorized to employ one additional clerk in each house at same rate as other clerks

153) 1851, March 3. Clause in appropriation act. Salary of any officer in any Territory of the United States not to be paid in any case where he shall absent himself from Territory and official duties for a period of time greater than sixty days.

154) 1852, May 4. Joint resolution approving act of Oregon assembly selecting Salem as seat of government, legalizing session of assembly held there.

155) 1852, May 19. Limit on mileage of delegate from Oregon removed.

156) 1852, June 15. If Territorial officer absent from Territory, no salary to be paid during that year, unless President certify that there was a good cause for it.

Previous act 153) modified, so that officer can receive salary if absent more than 60 days, if President certify it was for good cause. Does not apply to certain officers in Utah.

157) 1852, Aug. 31.   Clause in appropriation act. That if Territorial officer absent more than 60 days, he shall not be paid for time absent.

158) 1853, March 2.   Territory of Washington established. See pp. 42 and 43. Provisions copied from act for Oregon.

159) 1853, March 3.   New Mexico assembly authorized to employ a translator and interpreter and two clerks in addition for each house. Of four clerks for each house, two to be qualified to write in Spanish and two in English. Sessions to be limited to 60 days.

160) 1853, March 3.   Governor of New Mexico authorized to call extra session of assembly, not to exceed 90 days, and to be finished before first Monday of December, 1853.

161) 1854, Dec. 30.   GADSDEN PURCHASE. Treaty with Mexico. Ratifications exchanged June 30, 1854 ; proclaimed June 30, 1854. By which the United States acquired the tract of land now lying in the southern part of the Territories of New Mexico and Arizona, then in the Republic of Mexico and adjoining the United States south of the river Gila, and from the Rio Grand on the east to a point twenty miles below the mouth of the Gila on the west, on the Colorado river.

ARTICLE V.

" All the provisions of the 8th, 9th. 16th, and 17th articles of the Treaty of Guadalupe Hidalgo, shall apply to the Territory ceded by the Mexican Republic in the first article of the present treaty, and to all the rights of persons and property. both civil and ecclesiastical, within the same, as fully and effectually as if the said articles were herein again recited and set forth."

162) 1854, May 30.   Territories of Nebraska and Kansas established. See pp. 42, 43 and N. 20. Representation in legislatures may be increased in proportion to increase in population. Salaries : Governor, $2,500; secretary and judges, $2,000 each. Presiding officers in each house $3 extra. Chief clerk $4 and 3 other clerks $3 per day each. No one in army and navy to vote or hold office by reason of being in service therein.

163) 1854, July 27. Some changes in salaries. Judges in Oregon, Washington, Utah, and New Mexico, $2,500 ; in Minnesota, $2,000. Governor of New Mexico, $3,000. Secretary in Oregon, Washington, Utah and New Mexico, $2,000.

164) 1854, Aug. 2. District court of New Mexico to have jurisdiction over cases arising under revenue laws in county of El Paso in Texas and in New Mexico.

165) 1854, Aug. 4. The territory acquired from New Mexico by the Gadsden purchase incorporated in the Territory of New Mexico.

166) 1856, Feb. 11. Proclamation of President against persons attempting to control the political organization of Kansas by force.

167) 1856, May 15. Salary of governor of New Mexico $3,000 to be construed as full salary as governor and as superintendent of Indian affairs.

168) 1856, Aug. 16. Judges of Territorial supreme courts may fix times and places of their courts, in not more than three places in any one Territory. No officers of court to have witness fees. Each judge of Territorial supreme court to appoint one, and only one clerk for his district.

169) 1856, Aug. 18. Compensation, mileage, and contingent expenses of Minnesota legislature not to exceed sums previously appropriated therefor.

170) 1857, Feb. 26. Minnesota authorized to form constitution and State government.

171) 1857, March 3. In Oregon, Washington, Utah, and New Mexico the duties of superintendent of Indian affairs separated from those of governor. The salary of the governor of Washington was made the same as of the governor of Oregon; in Utah and New Mexico, $2,500.

172) 1858, June 5. President to appoint person or persons, who in conjunction with such persons appointed by the State of Texas to define boundaries between Texas and the Territories of the United States.

173) 1858, June 14. Judges of supreme court of each Territory may hold court in counties where by laws of Territory courts have already been established, to hear causes. except those in which the United States is a party, Provided, That the expense be paid by Territory or county and not by the United States.

174) 1860, May 26.   Same provision made in respect to California
                      as in 172).
175) 1861, Feb. 8.   Superintendent of Indian affairs for Wash-
                      ington.
176) 1861, Feb. 28.   Territory of Colorado organized, see pp. 42-
                      44 Governor given absolute veto. Council of
                      9, may be increased to 13, for two years. House
                      of 13 to 26 for one year. Apportionment
                      according to population except Indians. No ses-
                      sion over 40 days, except first of 60. No one hold-
                      ing commission under United States, except
                      postmasters, eligible to office. Salaries, &c., as
                      in 148).
177) 1861, March 2.   Territory of Nevada organized as in Colo-
                      rado.
178) 1861, March 2.   Territory of Dakota organized as in Colorado.
                      Certain portions of Utah and Washington added
                      to Nebraska.
179) 1861, May 21.   Session of Colorado Assembly postponed.
180) 1862, June 19.   Slavery forbidden in Territories, see p. 44.
181) 1862, July 1.   Bigamy forbidden in Territories, see p. 45.
                      Certain act of Utah, and all such acts counten-
                      ancing polygamy disapproved.
182) 1862, July 14.   Territorial limits of Nevada extended.
183) 1863, Feb. 9.   In Washington, district court to be held at
                      such times and places in districts (not exceeding
                      three places in each) as legislature shall deter-
                      mine. Until otherwise provided, to be held as
                      now.
184) 1863, Feb. 24.   Territory of Arizona organized, see pp. 42
                      to 44. Act differs from other organic acts.
                      Only three sections. First defines boundaries.
                      Second declares there shall be a governor;
                      council of 9, and a house of 18 ; a supreme court
                      of three judges, and inferior courts as the legis-
                      lature shall establish : also a secretary, marshal,
                      district attorney and a surveyor general ; the
                      last four and governor and judges to be
                      appointed by the President ; terms, powers,
                      duties, and compensation, and subordinate
                      officers as by the organic act of New Mexico :
                      acts amendatory thereto, and all legislative acts
                      of New Mexico to be in force in Arizona, unless
                      inconsistent with this, but no salaries to be
                      paid until officers enter on duties. Third pro-
                      vides that there shall be no slavery.

185) 1863, March 2.   Organic act for Colorado amended. Legislature may overrule governor's veto by a two-
thirds vote, and governor must return bill within three days.   Justices of the peace given
jurisdiction up to $300, and probate courts up to
$2,000.   Appeals allowed from probate courts
to Territorial supreme court.   In Dakota, governor's veto qualified same as above.

186) 1863, March 3.   That section of law of Nevada which requires
corporations owning property within the Terri-
tory but with principal place of business outside
it to remove office to the Territory, disapproved.
Any company, duly organized within any State
or Territory, may sue and be sued, etc., in
Nevada courts.

187) 1863, March 3.   District court of New Mexico given certain
jurisdiction over citizens of El Paso County,
Texas.

188) 1863, March 3.   Territory of Idaho organized, see pp. 42–44.
Further provisions as in 192).

189) 1864, March 21.   Nevada authorized to form constitution and
State government.

190) 1864, March 21.   Colorado authorized to form a constitution
and State government.

191) 1864, April 19.   Nebraska authorized to form a constitution
and State government.

192) 1864, May 26.   Territory of Montana organized, see pp. 42-
44.   Council of 7, may be increased to 13, for
two years House of 13, to 26 for one year.
Apportionment according to qualified voters.
Session's limit 40 days except first which may be
60.   Citizens qualified as in Idaho to vote at
first election.   Governor's veto can be overruled
by two-thirds vote.   Governor must return bill
within 3 days or it becomes law   Restrictions
that members of assembly not allowed to hold
office created during their term, etc., not to
apply to members of first assembly.   No one
holding appointment under United States,
except postmasters eligible to office.   Salaries :
Governor, $2,500; judges, $2,500; secretary,
$2,000.   Members of assembly $4 for attendance,
and $4 mileage. $4 per day to presiding officer
of each house.   Chief clerk, $4; five other
clerks, $3 each.   One session annually.   Gov-
ernor may call extraordinary session.   Assembly

to make no expenditure for objects not specially authorized in the appropriation acts of Congress, nor beyond the sums thus appropriated. Assembly to locate seat of government, which cannot be changed but by act of assembly, ratified at next election by majority of votes cast on question.
Portion of Territory of Idaho made part of Dakota.

193) 1864, June 17. Governor's veto in Washington may be overruled by two-thirds vote. Governor must return within 5 days, or it becomes law.

194) 1864, June 20. In Idaho governor may re-apportion for members of legislature, on basis of census to be taken. Rights of members elect not impaired. Date of election fixed.

195) 1866, April 10. Right of way granted to the Cascade Railroad Company, organized under laws of Washington Territory, and charter of said company declared valid.

196) 1866, June 29. Sessions of legislature of Washington to be biennial, see p. 43, N. 17. Members of council to be elected for 4 years, members of house for 2. To receive $6 per day instead of $3, mileage as now. An additional clerk allowed. Chief clerk to receive $6, and others $5. Time of first election for biennial session fixed. Act of legislature " in relation to Skamania county," disapproved.

197) 1866, July 26. Each judge of district court of Washington shall appoint clerk for his court, with same powers and subject to same provisions as clerk of supreme court of Territory.

198) 1867, Jan. 24. Regulating the elective franchise in the Territories, see p. 44.

199) 1867, March 2. Legislative assemblies and private charters, see p. 47. Probate courts in Montana to have jurisdiction in civil cases up to $500, and in criminal cases not requiring grand jury. No jurisdiction in land, nor in chancery or divorce causes. Judges to define districts, assign judges, and fix times and places of courts. Governor to determine election districts, and apportion representatives, but only for next election. Acts of legislative assembly of 1866, disapproved. Judges of Montana and Idaho to receive salary of $3,500, of all the other Territories, $2,500.

200) 1867, March 2.   In Idaho, judges to define districts and assign judges, and fix times and places of courts. Date of next session and of next election' fixed. Thereafter sessions and elections to be biennial. Members of house to be elected for two years, of council for four years. At next election one half of members of conncil to be elected for two years and one half for four.

201) 1867, March 2.   Jurisdiction of Territorial supreme courts in bankruptcy cases, see p. 45 and 133).

202) 1867, March 2.   Peonage abolished in New Mexico and United States.

203) 1867, March 26.   Resolution that laws passed by the last legislative assembly of New Mexico and signed by acting secretary and acting governor have full force and effect.

204) 1867, March 30.   Sessions of Colorado legislative assembly to be biennial. Members of council elected for four years, members of house for two. To receive $6 per day and mileage as now. May elect an additional clerk. Chief clerk to receive $6 per day, others $5.

205) 1868, July 20.   Proviso in appropriation act. The legislative assemblies to have biennial sessions after the first day of July next, see p. 46.

206) 1868, July 25.   Wyoming Territory organized, see p. 49. Council of 9, may be increased to 13, for two years. Members of house, 13 to 27, for one year. Act 198) incorporated in this act. Governor's veto can be overruled by two-thirds vote. Bill becomes law without governor's signature if he do not return it within five days, unless assembly adjourn. No limit on jurisdiction of probate courts. Salaries: governor, $2,000 as governor and $1,000 as superintendent of Indian affairs ; judges, $2,500 ; secretary, $1,800 ; members of assembly, $4 for attendance, and $3 mileage. General laws of Dakota in force until repealed by Wyoming assembly.

207) 1868, July 27.   Act of Washington assembly, "defining judicial districts and assigning judges," disapproved.

208) 1868, July 27.   In New Mexico, governor's veto may be overruled by two-thirds vote. Bill becomes law without governor's signature, if not returned

within three days, provided assembly does not in meantime adjourn. Secretary of New Mexico to be superintendent of public buildings and grounds, and receive $1,000 annually therefor. His duty to administer oath to members elect of both houses of legislature ; no one else competent unless secretary absent. His salary to be $2,000.

209) 1868, July 27.   Customs, etc., laws of the United States extended over Alaska. District court of Washington, with United States district courts of California and Oregon to have jurisdiction in all cases arising under these laws.

210) 1868, July 27.   Governor to assign district judges to districts in Utah, and appoint time and place of holding court, not more than two terms in each in one year.

211) 1869, March 1.   Representatives in Montana to be elected for two years, and sessions of assembly to be biennial.

212) 1869, March 3.   Clause in appropriation act, that sessions of Territorial assemblies be biennial, see p. 46.

213) 1869, March 3.   Clause in deficiency appropriation act, that salaries of Utah judges be the same as in Idaho and Montana. Another proviso, that salaries of judges of Wyoming do not commence until they have been commissioned and qualified.

214) 1869, March 3.   Date fixed for election of delegate in Washington and Idaho, and afterwards biennially on same date ; other officers elected at the same time to be elected at these dates, unless Territorial laws otherwise provide.

215) 1869, April 10.   Acts of New Mexico legislature imposing capitation tax on cattle introduced into Territory from other Territories or States or Mexico, disapproved and repealed.

216) 1869, March 3.   A railway and telegraph company ' existing under the laws of the Territory of Colorado," recognized by this act.

217) 1869, March 3.   Walla-Walla and Columbia River Railroad Company, a corporation under laws of Washington, "and duly incorporated" granted right of way. County commissioners of Walla-Walla may subscribe to stock, after it has been approved by three-fourths vote of people of county at special election.

218) 1870, March 23. Apportionment of members of Arizona assembly in 1866, 1867, and 1868, by the governor declared valid. Date of next election for all officers fixed. Apportionment by governor. Date of session of assembly fixed. Justices of peace not to have jurisdiction in land cases or where amount be over $300.

219) 1870, April 28. Boundary between State of Nebraska and Territory of Dakota re-defined.

220) 1870, May 4. Appeals from probate courts in Colorado to district court and not directly to supreme court. General assembly by general laws, authorized to incorporate for charitable or educational purposes.

221) 1870, June 17. Salaries of Judges in all Territories, $3,000.

222) 1870, June 30. On the jurisdiction of Territorial courts in bankruptcy.

223) 1870, July 1. Two sections of an act of Wyoming assembly "for the collection of taxes," and eleven sections of an act "to create and regulate corporations," disapproved.

224) 1870, July 8 Congress incorporates the United States Freehold Land and Emigration Company in Colorado and New Mexico.

225) 1870, July 14. Portion of a statute of New Mexico legislature disapproved.

226) 1870, July 14. Writs of error allowed from probate court in Colorado to supreme court of Territory.

227) 1870, July 15. Laws of Idaho assembly taxing Chinamen, etc. disapproved. Act creating district attorney in each county disapproved. Acts giving extra pay to officers paid by the United States disapproved.

228) 1870, Dec. 13. Probate courts in Idaho to have jurisdiction up to $500, and in criminal cases not requiring a grand jury, but not in land, chancery, or divorce cases. Appeals to lie from probate courts to the district court.

229) 1870, Dec. 15. Right of way granted to Utah Central Railroad, a corporation created under laws of Utah.

230) 1871, Feb. 21. Apportionment of members of assembly of Colorado to be made by governor, chief justice and United States attorney.

231) 1871, Feb. 21. Apportionment act of legislature of Wyoming disapproved.

232) 1871, April 20. Date of session of New Mexico legislature fixed, and election ordered.

233) 1872, Feb. 2. No State to be admitted to the Union without having the necessary population to entitle it to one Representative.

234) 1872, May 8. Clause in appropriation act. Expense for printing for any session of the legislature of any Territory not to exceed $4,000.

235) 1872, May 9. In Washington and Idaho, date of election of delegates fixed, and to be biennial thereafter; and all elective officers to be elected at these times, unless otherwise ordered by Territorial law.

236) 1872, May 8. Clause in deficiency appropriation act taking away extra salary given to secretary of New Mexico as superintendent of public buildings, see 208).

237) 1872, May 27. Act of Dakota assembly disapproved, except so far as Dakota Southern Railroad Company may profit by it.

238) 1872, June 1. Right of way granted to Dakota Grand Trunk Railway Company, corporation organized under laws of Dakota. Nothing in this to be construed as recognizing or denying authority of Dakota legislature to create railroad corporations.

239) 1872, June 1. Utah, Idaho, and Montana Railroad Company, a corporation organized under laws of Utah, legalized and made valid. Does not recognize or deny right of governor and legislature of Utah to create railroad corporations.

240) 1872, June 8. In any of the Territories, if vacancy occur during recess of council in office which is filled by appointment of governor, with consent of council, governor alone may grant commission to expire at end of next session of council.

241) 1872, June 8. Right of way granted to Denver and Rio Grande Railway Company, a corporation created under laws of Colorado. This does not affirm or deny right of a Territory to incorporate a railroad company.

242) 1872, June 8. Right of way granted to New Mexico and Gulf Railway Company. Does not affirm or deny right of a Territory to incorporate a railroad company.

243) 1872, June 10. Territorial legislatures permitted to incor-

porate for certain purposes by general laws, see p. 48.

244) 1872, Dec. 24. Supreme court of Arizona may hold adjourned terms.

245) 1873, Jan. 16. Clerks and marshals of United States courts not to practice as attorneys, etc., in any court for which they are acting as officers.

246) 1873, Jan. 16. Provisions of act forbidding members of Congress to receive pay for services before any department, commission, etc., where United States a party, extended to delegates from Territories.

247) 1873, Jan. 23. Sessions of Territorial assemblies limited, see p. 46. Members to receive $6 per day, during sessions, and mileage as now. President of council and speaker of house to receive $10 per day, chief clerk $8, seven other officers $5 each. Governors $3,500, secretaries $2,500.

247a) 1873, Feb. 17. Certain portion of Dakota attached to Montana.

248) 1873, March 1. Secretary of the Interior to have powers and perform duties in relation to Territories now by law or custom exercised and performed by Secretary of State.

249) 1873, March 3. Clause in appropriation act re-enacting last part of act 247). In appropriation for Washington proviso that sessions shall not extend beyond forty days.

250) 1873, March 3. Apportionment for election of members of Wyoming legislature to be made by governor.

251) 1873, March 3. Right of way granted to Utah Northern Railroad Company, corporation organized under laws of Utah. This does not recognize or deny authority of Utah legislature to create railroad corporations.

252) 1873, Dec. 1. The Revised Statutes, embracing the statutes of the United States in force on the first of December, 1873, as revised and consolidated by commissioners appointed under act of Congress. Containing nothing new,—a compilation of the laws still in force. Enacted June 22, 1874.

253) 1874, April 7. Not necessary in Territorial courts to exercise separately the common-law and chancery jurisdictions vested in them, but no party shall be deprived of right of trial by jury in cases

cognizable at common-law, and how the appellate jurisdiction of the Supreme Court of the United States over the Territorial courts is to be exercised.

254) 1874, May 27. County commissioners of Thurston county, Washington empowered to issue bonds to construct a railroad. Contract must be ratified by a two-thirds vote of citizens of the county.

255) 1874, June 20. Clause in appropriation act : duty of secretary of each Territory to furnish to Secretary of Treasury estimate of lawful expenses each year.

256) 1874, June 20. Apportionment for election of members of Wyoming legislature to be made by governor. This power to be retained by governor until legislature make an apportionment.

257) 1874, June 22. Clause in the deficiency appropriation act, that no extraordinary session of legislature of any Territory, wherever authorized by law, shall be called until President have approved reason for it.

258) 1874, June 22. District courts substituted for supreme courts as bankruptcy courts in the Territories.

259) 1874, June 23. In relation to the courts of Utah, see pp. 49 and 50. United States marshal to attend all sessions of supreme and district courts, and serve all processes. United States attorney to attend all courts of record and prosecute all criminal cases. To be two terms of supreme and four of district court each year. Jurisdiction of district courts : exclusive original in chancery proceedings, in all actions at law where amount is over $300, and in land and mining questions ; jurisdiction in divorce. Jurisdiction of probate courts : in settlement of. estates, matters of guardianship, etc., but no other civil, chancery, or criminal jurisdiction ; with district courts concurrent jurisdiction in suits of divorce for statutory causes. Justices of the peace to have jurisdiction up to $300. Appeals from justices of the peace and probate courts to district courts. A writ of error from United States Supreme Court to Territorial supreme court in criminal cases where sentenced to capital punishment or convicted of polygamy. Provisions on qualification and selection of jurors. Terri-

torial supreme court to appoint commissioners to take acknowledgments of bail, as United States circuit court commissioners ; and to have same authority as examining and committing magistrates in Territorial cases as now possessed by justices of the peace. Governor to appoint notaries public for each county ; and Territorial act " concerning notaries public " be approved, except...... Territorial act "in relation to marshals and attorneys," disapproved. Act of Congress of 1853, "regulating fees, etc., to marshals and attorneys, etc.," extended over Utah, but district attorney not to receive in all more than $3,500.

260) 1875, March 2. Declaring the true intent and meaning of an
      •   act of Dakota legislature relating to homesteads.

261) 1875, March 3. Colorado to form constitution and State government.

262) 1876, March 3. Amendment to the above act.

263) 1876, April 14. Undetermined bankruptcy cases in supreme courts of Territories to be transferred to the district courts thereof.

264) 1876, May 1. Clause in deficiency appropriation act : Salaries of Territorial officers to commence only when they have taken the proper oath and entered on their duties ; oath to be administered in the Territory in which office is held.

265) 1876, June 29. Revised Statutes amended so as to permit appeals from the Territorial supreme court of Washington to the Supreme Court of the United States in cases where the laws of the United States, as well as the Constitution, come in question.

266) 1876, July 19. Arizona legislature authorized to overrule governor's veto by two-thirds vote. Governor must return bill in 10 days, or it becomes law, unless legislature have adjourned.

267) 1876, Aug. 15. Clause in appropriation act, fixing date of sessions of legislature of Montana.

268) 1878, March 16. In United States and Territorial Courts accused persons may testify.

269) 1878, June 8. Previous provision that Territorial legislatures should not grant private charters, or especial privileges, does not prohibit them from creating municipal corporations, and conferring

on them the necessary administrative powers, either by general or special acts.

270) 1878, June 19. Clause in appropriation act, see p. 47. The several legislatures to divide their Territories into as many districts as they desire, as equal as may be according to population, except Indians not taxed. Number of districts not to exceed number of members. Subordinate officers allowed in each legislature: chief clerk $6 per day; two clerks $5; two at $4: chaplain at $1.50. No greater number of officers or charges allowed, except secretary may receive fees for official duties imposed by legislature not in the organic act.

271) 1879, Feb. 3. Act of New Mexico assembly incorporating the Society of the Jesuit Fathers disapproved, "because it is an act of incorporation with especial privileges."

272) 1879, Feb. 15. Any woman member of the bar of the highest court of any State or Territory to be admitted to practice before the Supreme Court of the United States.

273) 1879, March 3. Additional supreme court judge for Dakota. A fourth judicial district defined. New judge to have no jurisdiction in causes where United States a party.

274) 1879, June 27. Provisions of act 270) not to shorten tenure of office of members of present assemblies.

275) 1880, April 16. In any Territory lawful to fill vacancy in office of justice of peace by appointment or election, as provided by governor and assembly of such Territory, to hold office until successor regularly elected and qualified.

276) 1880, June 3. In Montana, Idaho, and Wyoming, the governor and speaker of house and president of council of last session, to act as board of apportionment. To re-apportion in their respective Territories on the basis of the last census of 1880. Election to be held. Legislature so elected may alter the re-apportionment. Members of boards of apportionment to receive same compensation per day and mileage as allowed to presiding officers of the Territorial legislatures.

277) 1880, Dec. 23. Revised statutes amended to limit the sessions of Territorial legislatures to sixty days.

278) 1881, Dec. 21.   Election of New Mexico legislatures legalized. 276) made applicable to New Mexico.

279) 1882, March 22.   Revised statutes relating to bigamy in Territories amended, see p. 49. Each house after election to have power to decide on elections and qualifications of its members.

280) 1882, Aug 5.   Clause in appropriation act. Printing expenses of any session of any Territorial legislature not to exceed $3,750. In Montana, board appointed in 276)—with chief justice added—to organize new county.

281) 1882, Aug. 7.   Any vacancy arising under 279) from failure to elect to be filled by governor.

282) 1882, Aug. 7.   Act of Congress of Feb. 26, 1853 regulating fees of attorney etc., extended to New Mexico and Arizona, *cf.* 259).

283) 1883, Jan. 10.   Revised Statutes amended to extend jurisdiction of justices of peace in Washington, Idaho, and Montana to $300.

284) 1883, March 3.   Revised Statutes amended so as not to exclude retired army officers from holding civil office in Territories.

285) 1884, Feb. 14.   Proviso in deficiency appropriation act, That legislative proceedings, records and laws of New Mexico shall be printed in English. An election in New Mexico declared valid. Date of session fixed, not to exceed 40 days.

Validation

286) 1884, June 12.   Dakota legislature to have 24 members of council and 48 of house. Apportionment made accordingly.

287) 1884, July 4.   Two additional supreme court justices for Dakota (6). Five a quorum. 5th district not to have jurisdiction where United States a party. For that purpose a part of 2d district. 6th district to have all jurisdiction.

An additional supreme justice for Washington. Three a quorum, but no justice to act in appeals from his own decision.

288) 1884, July 5.   Ten acts of Washington assembly, in spite of defects and irregularities, validated.

289) 1885, Jan. 28.   Jurisdiction of Wyoming justices of peace limited to $300.

290) 1885, March 3.   Revised Statutes relating to power of Territorial legislatures to incorporate for certain purposes, amended so as to include banks and canals.

291) 1885, March 3.   Clause in appropriation act authorizing Dakota legislature to redistrict Territory.

292) 1885 March 3.   Appeals or writs of error from Territorial supreme courts to Supreme Court of United States, allowed only when amount over $5,000. Does not apply to cases involving validity of patents or copyrights, or of treaty or statute or authority exercised under United States.

293) 1886, Jan. 19.   Election of Wyoming legislature legalized. Governor, secretary and president of council act as board of apportionment for next legislature. To reapportion on basis of voting population. 276) to apply for election and compensation.

294) 1886, June 19.   Columbia County, Washington Territory authorized to issue bonds ($40,000) for building of county court house in accordance with vote of the people of said county at election in November, 1884.

295) 1886, June 30.   General laws of Dakota for incorporation of insurance companies, declared valid, and companies incorporated under them legal.

296) 1886, July 10.   Additional supreme judge for Montana. Provisions same as in act 287), for Washington.

297) 1886, July 30.   Act relating to power of incorporating and passing of special acts, by Territorial legislatures, see p. 48. Nothing in this abridges power of Congress to annul any law of Territory,

298) 1887, Feb. 8.   Act providing for allotment of lands in severalty to Indians. No Territory shall pass or enforce any law denying to any Indian within its jurisdiction to whom such allotment has been made the equal protection of the law.

299) 1887, Feb. 28.   Additional supreme judge for New Mexico. Present supreme court to make new division of Territory and assign judges. No other change, except three judges constitute a quorum.

300) 1887, March 3.   Alien persons and corporations prohibited from acquiring real estate in Territories, except by inheritance, or in collection of debts heretofore created. Prohibition does not apply where right is secured to foreign persons by treaty. Corporations having more than 20 per cent. of stock owned by aliens prohibited from acquiring real estate in Territories. No corporation, except railway, canal, or turnpike, to own more

than 5.000 acres of land in any of the Territories; and no railroad, canal, or turnpike corporation shall acquire more than is necessary
for its proper operation. Does not affect title
to lands now lawfully held. Property in viola-
tion to this to be forfeited to United States.

301) 1887, March 3. Anti-Polygamy Act. Laws of Utah that
prosecutions for adultery can only be on com-
plaint of husband or wife annulled. Commissioners in Utah to have all power and
jurisdiction of justices of peace. Marriage
ceremonies in Territories require certifi-
cate. Laws of Utah allowing illegitimate
children to inherit annulled. Laws of Utah
conferring further jurisdiction on probate courts
annulled. Laws of Utah and of so-called State
of Deseret creating Perpetual Emigrating Fund
Company annulled; corporation dissolved; legislature forbidden to create any such corporation. Incorporation of Mormon Church likewise
dissolved. Laws of Utah providing for election
of probate judges by legislature annulled; to be
appointed by President. Female votes prohibited in Utah, laws to that effect annulled.
Legislative laws for voting annulled. Districts
and apportionments abolished. Commissioners
to redistrict and apportion. Oath to be taken
before voting or holding office. Polygamists
prohibited. State of Deseret laws for militia
annulled.

302) 1888, June 25. Additional supreme judge for Utah. Three
a quorum, but no judge to sit on writ of error
or appeal from his own decision. Temporarily
the additional judge to be assigned by governor to any of the districts to act as associate
of the judge there presiding.

303) 1888, July 19. Act of New Mexico legislature creating San
Juan county ratified. Nothing in act 297) to be
construed as prohibiting Territorial legislatures
from creating new counties and locating county
seats thereof.

304) 1888, July 23. Issue of bonds by New Mexico legislature ratified. Tax to be levied in each county to raise
a sinking fund.

305) 1888, Aug. 9. Two additional supreme judges for Dakota
(making eight in all). Five to be a quorum.

No judge to sit on supreme court in trial of question decided by him in his district, or in which he has any interest. New judicial districts fixed. All district courts to have full jurisdiction.

306) 1889, Feb. 22.   Dakota to be divided   North Dakota, South Dakota, Montana and Washington authorized to form constitutions and State governments.

307) 1889, March 2.   Clause in deficiency appropriation act, That next assembly of Wyoming may provide by law for subsequent legislatures to convene on fixed day in January on years following general elections.

308) 1890, May 15.   Location of County seat, Shoshone County, Idaho, to be submitted to vote of people.

309) 1890, May 2.   Territory of Oklahoma organized, see p. 49. Council 13, house 26, first session 120 days. Seven counties established and county seats, but legislature may provide for changing latter. At first election people of each county may vote for name of same. Apportionment by governor. Representation in ratio of population (except Indians not taxed). Members of legislature shall be inhabitants of district for which elected. Governor may convene extraordinary session at any time. Right of suffrage and holding office at subsequent elections to be fixed by legislature, but no one in army or navy to be allowed to vote by reason of being in service in Territory and no one in army or navy to hold office. Governor's veto can be overruled by two-thirds vote. He must return bill within five days. Justices of peace jurisdiction up to $100. Certain laws of Nebraska to be in force until after first session of legislature. Governor and assembly to locate seat of government subject to change by same. Not required to submit laws to Congress for approval.

310) 1890, May 16.   Act of Idaho legislature to provide for a certain wagon road ratified.

311) 1890, June 25.   Funding act of revised statutes of Arizona amended and approved.

312) 1890, July 2.   Marshals and district attorneys of New Mexico and Arizona allowed to retain fees up to $6,000.

313) 1890, July 10.   Additional associate justice for New Mexico.

Three a quorum. No judge to sit at hearing on appeal from his own decision. Judges to redistrict.

314) 1891, Feb. 11.   Additional associate justices for Arizona same as 313), but legislature may alter districts.

315) 1891, March 3.   Circuit Court of Appeals created and given same appellate jurisdiction over Territorial supreme courts as over district and circuit courts.

316) 1891, March 3.   Act for the protection of lives of miners in the organized and unorganized Territories.

317) 1891, March 3   Clause in appropriation act: Probate courts in Oklahoma given such jurisdiction in town site matters as granted in Kansas.

318) 1892, Feb. 11.   Governor and legislature authorized to establish a fourth judicial district in Utah.

319) 1892, March 18.   Act of Arizona legislature making appropriation for display at Columbian Exposition ratified.

320) 1892, July 13.   Funding act of Arizona amended, see 311).

321) 1892, July 16.   Proviso in appropriation act that commissioners in Utah shall be residents.

322) 1892, July 28.   Clause in appropriation act. Governor and two others appointed commissions in Oklahoma to apportion Territory into 13 council and 26 representative districts, according to population. Date fixed on which governor to proclaim an election for delegate, members of assembly, and county and township officers. County commissioners to be county canvassing board. Governor, secretary, and Territorial auditor to be Territorial canvassing board. Assembly elected under this act not to consider any proposition or pass any bill to remove seat of government from present location.

323) 1892, Aug. 3.   In eight States and the Territories of New Mexico, Utah, and Arizona fees of jurors and witnesses in United States Courts fixed. Provision against double mileage fees being paid.

324) 1893, March 3.   Clause in appropriation act, relative to duties of commissioners appointed under 279).

325) 1893, Oct. 17.   In Oklahoma, all male citizens of United States, 21 years of age, actual residents on Oct. 21, 1893, and 30 days prior thereto, of that portion of Territory opened by proclamation of President, Sept. 16, 1893,—known as Cherokee

Outlet—shall be entitled to vote and hold office at first municipal elections held in said Cherokee Outlet for the organization of city, village and town government.

326) 1893, Dec. 21. Two additional associate justices of the supreme Court of Oklahoma. Three judges must concur to reverse a decision of the district court.

327) 1894, Feb. 21. Salt Lake City, Utah, may become indebted to 6% on value of taxable property at last assessment. All bonds and obligations in excess of that void.

328) 1894, July 16. Act to enable Utah; to form constitution and State government.

329) 1894, July 18. Authorizing county of Coconino, Arizona, to issue bonds for the construction of a county building at the county seat.

330) 1894, July 31. Clause in appropriation act. In Oklahoma, governor to appoint commission to apportion Territory for members of legislature. Date of election after such apportionment fixed. Legislature thus elected not to consider proposition to remove Territorial seat of government from present location.

331) 1894, Aug. 3. Act to amend section 15 of act approving with amendments the Funding Act of Arizona approved June 25, 1890. (Extends indebtedness which may be funded).

APPENDIX C.

DISTRICT OF COLUMBIA.

The Constitution of the United States (Article I, Section 8, seventeenth clause), declares that Congress shall have power :

"To exercise exclusive legislation in all cases whatsoever, over such district (not exceeding ten miles square) as may, by cession of particular States, and the acceptance of Congress, become the seat of government of the United States."

In pursuance of this provision, Maryland and Virginia[1] made cessions which were accepted by Congress and the permanent seat of government was established by an act of July 16, 1790, and an act to amend the same of March 3, 1791. By the act "concerning the District of Columbia," of February 27, 1801, Congress assumed complete jurisdiction over the district.

Until 1871 the government of the district of Columbia was of the ordinary municipal character, resting upon charters granted by Congress to the cities of Washington and Georgetown. In 1871, the experiment was tried of creating a Territorial government. The act was passed February 21, 1871.

By this act the District was "constituted a body corporate for municipal purposes." and was given a government in most respects like that established in the other Territories. There was a governor and a secretary, both appointed by the President and given the usual powers and duties. There was a legislature of two houses, the upper apppointed by the President and the lower elected by the people. And the people were authorized to elect a delegate to represent the District in Congress. There was also a board of public works, charged with certain strictly municipal duties.

This Territorial government was given power to raise money by tax and loan. It rushed at once into a very extensive system of public improvements, which resulted in a debt of $20,000,000, on an assessed valuation of less than $80,000.[2] The Territorial government was accordingly abolished by an act of June 20, 1874. This provided for the appointment of a Board of Commissioners, who were given "all the power and authority now lawfully vested in the governor or the board of public works." Since that date the government of the District of Columbia has been administered by Congress through this Board.

---

1. Virginia's cession retroceded in 1846.
2. Johnston : Lalor's Political Cyclopædia, The National Capitol.

BIBLIOGRAPHY.

ADAMS, HENRY. History of the United States. 9 vols. ⌐
New York, 1889-91.

ADAMS, H. B. Maryland's Influence on Western Land
Cessions to the United States. John Hopkins
University Studies, Third Series, No. 1.

ALBACH, J. R. Annals of the West. Pittsburgh, 1858.

BANCROFT, GEORGE History of the United States of
America. 6 vols. New York, 1883.

BENTON, T. H. See United States. Congressional Debates.

BURNET, JACOB. Notes on the Early Settlement of the
Northwestern Territory. . New York and Cincinnati, 1847.

BRYCE, JAMES. The American Commonwealth, Third
Edition, 2 vols. New York, 1893 and 1895.

CARR, LUCIEN. Missouri. A Bone of Contention. Boston, 1888.

CHASE, S. P. Statutes of Ohio and of the Northwestern Territory. Cincinnati, 1833.

CLAIBORNE, J. F. H. Mississippi as a Province, Territory
and State. 1880.

COLES, EDWARD. History of the Ordinance of 1787. Philadelphia, 1856.

COOLEY, T. M. Michigan. A History of Governments.
Boston, 1885.

CURTIS, G T. Constitutional History of the United States.
Vol. 1. New York, 1889.

CUTLER, W. P. AND J. P. Life, Journals and Correspondence of Rev. Manasseh Cutler. 2 vols. Cincinnati, 1888.

DONALDSON, THOMAS. The Public Domain. Its History
with Statistics. Washington, 1884.

DOUGLAS, S. A. Popular Sovereignty in the Territories.
Harper's New Monthly Magazine. September,
1859.

Dunn, J. P., Jr   Indiana. A Redemption from Slavery. Boston, 1888.

Fiske, John.   The Critical Period of American History. Boston, 1889.

Force, Peter.   History of the Ordinance of 1787. National Intelligencer, August 26, 1847.

Gannett, Henry.   Boundaries of the United States, and of the Several States and Territories. Washington, 1885.

Garrett, W. R.   History of the South Carolina Cession. Nashville, 1884.

Haywood, John.   Civil and Political History of Tennessee. Knoxville, 1823.

Hildreth, Richard.   History of the United States of America. First Series, 3 vols. Second Series, 3 vols. New York, 1849 and 1852.

Hinsdale, B. A.   The Old Northwest. New York, 1888.

Johnston, Alexander.   Articles on United States History in Lalor's Political Cyclopædia.

Johnston, Alexander.   History of American Politics. New York, 1889

King, Rufus.   Ohio. First Fruits of the Ordinance of 1787. Boston, 1891.

Lalor, J. J.   Cyclopædia of Political Science, Political Economy and of the Political History of the United States. 3 vols. Chicago, 1884.

Mason, E. C.   The Veto Power. Boston, 1891.

McMaster, J. B.   History of the People of the United States. Vols. I-IV. New York, 1883-1895.

Michigan Pioneer and Historical Society Collections. Vol. II. 1888.

Neill, E. D.   History of Minnesota. Philadelphia, 1858.

Phelan, James.   History of Tennessee. The Making of a State. Boston, 1888.

Pickett, A. J.   History of Alabama. 2 vols. Charleston, 1851.

Pomeroy, J. N.   Introducton to the Constitutional Law of the United States. Tenth edition. Revised by E. H. Bennett, Boston, 1888.

POOLE, W. F. Dr. Cutler and the Ordinance of 1787.
North American Review, No. 251. April, 1786.

POORE, BEN. PERLEY The Federal and State Constitutions, Colonial Charters, and Other Organic Laws of the United States. Second Edition. 2 vols. Washington, 1878.

RAMSEY, J. G. M. Annals of Tennessee. Philadelphia, 1853.

RHODES, J. F. History of the United States from the Compromise of 1850. 2 vols. New York, 1893.

ROOSEVELT, THEODORE. The Winning of the West. New York, 1889

ROYCE, JOSIAH. California. A Study of American Character. Boston, 1886.

SATO, SHOSUKE. History of the Land Question in the United States. Johns Hopkins University Studies. Fourth Series, Nos. 7, 8 and 9.

SCHOULER, JAMES. History of the United States. 5 vols. Washington, 1880-1889.

SPRING, L. W. Kansas. The Prelude to the War for the Union. Boston, 1885.

STORY, JOSEPH. Commentaries on the Constitution of the United States. Fourth Edition. Notes by T. M. Cooley. 2 vols. Boston, 1873.

STROUD, G. M. A Sketch of the Laws Relating to Slavery in the Several States of the United States of America. Second Edition. Philadelphia, 1856.

UNITED STATES. American State Papers. Miscellaneous. Vols. I. and II.

UNITED STATES. Annals of Congress, 1789-1823.

UNITED STATES. Congressional Debates. 1823 - 1837. Abridgment of same, by Benton, T. H. Washington, 1857-1861.

UNITED STATES. Congressional Globe, 1833-1873.

UNITED STATES. Congressional Record, 1873-1894.

UNITED STATES. Reports of Committees of Senate; of House.

UNITED STATES. Statute at Large, 1789-1873. 17 vols. Little, Brown & Co. Boston.

UNITED STATES. Revised Statutes. 1874. Washington.

UNITED STATES. Supplement to Revised Statutes. Washington.

UNITED STATES. Statutes at Large, 1873-1894.

— VON HOLST, H. Constitutional and Political History of the United States 7 vols. Chicago, 1887-1892.

WADE, D. S. Self-Government in the Territories. The International Review. March, 1879.

WILLIAMS, G. W. History of the Negro Race in America. New York.

WILSON, Henry. History of the Rise and Fall of the Slave Power in America. 3 vols. Boston, 1877.

WINSOR, JUSTIN. Narrative and Critical History of America. Vol. VII., Appendix. Boston, 1888.

* 9 7 8 3 7 4 4 7 2 1 5 2 3 *